D0680494

COMMUNICATION, ORGANIZATION, AND CHANGE WITHIN A FEMINIST CONTEXT

A Participant Observation of A Feminist Collective

Lynette J. Eastland

The Edwin Mellen Press
Lewiston/Queenston/Lampeter

BOWLING GREEN STATE
UNIVERSITY LIBRARIES

Library of Congress Cataloging-in-Publication Data

Eastland, Lynette J.
    Communication, organization, and change within a feminist context
    : a participant observation of a feminist collective / Lynette J.
    Eastland.
        p.   cm.
    Includes bibliographical references (p.   ).
    ISBN 0-88946-121-X
    1. Women-owned business enterprises--Utah--Salt Lake City.
    2. Bookstores--Utah--Salt Lake City. 3. Coffeehouses--Utah--Salt
    Lake City. 4. Feminists--Utah--Salt Lake City. 5. Lesbians--Utah-
    -Salt Lake City. 6. Twenty Rue Jacob (Organization) I. Title.
    HD6072.6.U52S254 1991
    338.6'422--dc20   91-31400
                                                                          CIP

ISBN 0-88946-121-X

A CIP catalog record for this book
is available from the British Library.

Copyright © 1991 Lynette J. Eastland

All rights reserved. For information contact

The Edwin Mellen Press   The Edwin Mellen Press
        Box 450   Box 67
Lewiston, New York   Queenston, Ontario
    USA 14092   CANADA L0S 1L0

The Edwin Mellen Press, Ltd.
        Lampeter, Dyfed, Wales
    UNITED KINGDOM SA48 7DY

Printed in the United States of America

To my mother,

Joy Seccombe Eastland,

who would have been very proud,

To Abby, in whose heart Twenty Rue Jacob was born, and

To Mickey, who first shared this dream with me.

TABLE OF CONTENTS

INTRODUCTION

The focus of this study is the communicative acts which occur among members of a collective of women who own and operate a feminist business located in Salt Lake City, Utah and their clients. The business, a bookstore and coffeehouse, serves as the primary gathering place or community center for feminists, and particularly lesbian feminists, in the area.

This particular type of organizational setting is unique. It is regarded by the feminist members as an enactment of feminist ideology and therefore organizational action can be regarded as productions of feminist ideology. My purpose in this dissertation is to examine the interactions of the collective to gain an understanding of the dialectical relationship between the ideology of the organization and organizational action. I want to explicate the means by which the ideology is created, sustained, modified, and enacted by organizational participants, and to examine how ideology leads to and helps explain action in an organizational setting. An examination of naturally occurring talk in this organization can contribute to an understanding of the relationship between ideology and organizational action in general

and the enactment of feminism in an organizational
setting in particular.

The talk was collected in three primary settings.
Structured meetings occurred in private homes of
individual collective members. They are scheduled as
needed and vary in frequency from monthly, when not
much is going on or people are gone, to several times a
week when there is a crisis. An agenda is drawn up at
the beginning of the meeting with time periods allotted
to individual agenda items. During times of crisis,
however, the agenda may be abandoned and the meeting
may last until late into the night.

The second type of setting in which business talk
occurs is social. Inasmuch as collective members are
also friends, they regularly talk to one another at
dinners in each other's homes, attend parties, or go on
weekend trips together. Conversation in this setting
is often related to business matters, feminist or
lesbian feminist issues and, in fact, new ideas or
crises are often initially introduced or informally
dealt with within a social context.

The third setting is the business setting. This
involves business-related talk between collective
members or collective members and customers that occurs
in the work setting. Collective members are rarely
assigned times they have to be in the place of business
(although this has not always been the case), but
instead come and go at will. Some spend significant
parts of every day there, while others drop by only
occasionally or come in during closed hours to work on
books or stock the supplies. Time spent at the store
is perceived as an indication of commitment and women
who limit their time there are often the subject of
complaint by some collective members.

I had access to the naturally occurring discourse of this collective of women because I spent two and a half years as a participant observer in the coffee-house-bookstore. Sometimes I took fieldnotes while in the business, sometimes I reconstructed events soon after they had concluded, sometimes I conducted unstructured interviews. Sometimes I even taped and later transcribed meetings or interviews.

But my "data" for this study encompass more than these observations. I also include much of the feminist literature on feminist ideology and organization (a literature that many of the organizational members were familiar with), inasmuch as that literature provides an intellectual and social context for the naturally occurring discourse. In addition, I also use as data my own personal experiences and responses to the observations I made. In a sense, over two and a half years of participant observation, I became one of my own 'key informants.' Thus, the data base for this study is rich and varied, and the analytic task first requires a sense of how these data can be productively exploited. The thinking of Clifford Geertz in this regard is most helpful.

Clifford Geertz, in his 1980 article, "Blurred Genres," addresses what he refers to as the refiguration of social thought. "Something is happening," says Geertz, "to the way we think about the way we think."[1] The lines of division between disciplines are no longer distinct, and social (or behavioral or human or cultural) scientists have become free to "shape their work in terms of its necessities rather than received ideas to what they ought or ought not be doing."[2]

This shift in thought is evident in changes in the instruments of reasoning. Theory, Geertz contends, moves mainly by analogy, ("a seeing-as comprehension of the less intelligent by the more,"[3]) and it is the changes in the metaphors we use for understanding society that the shift in thought is evident. Society, says Geertz, is "less and less represented as an elaborate machine or a quasi-organism than as a serious game, a sidewalk drama, or a behavioral text."[4]

It is the notion of behavioral text that is most useful to me in defining and delineating the focus of this study. The text analogy is, to Geertz, the broadest and most venturesome of the recent refigurations of social theory.[5] The notion of social action as text is seated in Paul Ricoeur's concept of inscription, the fixation of meaning. Geertz explains:

> When we speak, our utterances fly by as events like any other behavior; unless what we say is inscribed in writing (or some other established recording process), it is as evanescent as what we do.
> If it is inscribed or recorded in some way, it still passes, but for a time anyway, its meaning - the said not the saying - to a degree and for awhile remains.[6]

This is true for action in general; meaning can persist in a way its actuality cannot.

In this study, then, I am acting as the inscriber, recording both the talk and the social action so that I might from them extrapolate the meaning from the perspective of the organizational participants. But because my data are broader than just the recorded

observations of talk and social action, my notion of
text encompasses more than the talk and action. Thus,
I am also using as text: the physical space of the
business, the texts of the organization (signs, news-
letters, etc.), my personal experiences and responses
to the observations I made as a participant observer in
the business, and feminist literature on feminist
ideology and organization. I take it as my analytic
task to integrate the varied texts to provide an understanding or interpretation of the way in which feminist
ideology and organizational action play themselves out
dialectically in this particular organizational
setting. This inscribed text functions as the
empirical data and this study is a critical analysis of
it.

Chapter One includes a discussion of the
theoretical description and the methodological
assumptions of this study. A definition of ideology,
grounded in an examination of traditional approaches to
ideology in organizations and a discussion of ideology
and feminism, is provided.

Chapter Two provides a context for the analysis by
discussing the historical development of the business
and describing the organizational setting and
clientele. An explication of the concept of feminist
business enables the reader to understand the unique
relationship between ideology and action in such
organizations.

Chapters Three, Four and Five contain an analysis
of the data centering around three specific ideological
components which emerged in the data: 1) sisterhood,
2) politicalism and 3) separatism. The analysis is
grounded in a theoretical discussion of each component.

Examples or 'productions' of ideology will be the focus of the analysis.

Chapter Six discusses the findings in terms of the implications for the study of ideology in organizations in general and feminist organizations in specific.

An ethnographic description of a typical day in the organizational setting is provided in an appendix.

INTRODUCTION

NOTES

[1]Clifford Geertz, "Blurred Genres: The Refiguration of Social
Thought," <u>American Scholar</u> (Spring 1980) p. 166.

[2]Clifford Geertz, p. 167.

[3]Clifford Geertz, p. 168.

[4]Clifford Geertz, p. 168.

[5]Clifford Geertz, p. 174.

[6]Clifford Geertz, p. 175.

CHAPTER I

THEORY AND METHODOLOGY

Clifford Geertz's observations on the blurring of disciplinary genres are certainly apt commentaries on the scholarly study of organizations. As Mary Strine and Michael Pacanowsky note:

> Ten years ago, perhaps no other 'social science' was as determinedly positivistic or functionalistic. Today, perhaps no other social study is as agonizingly self-conscious about the pitfalls of a narrowed conception of scholarship and the potentials of alternative views (see, for example, Weich, 1979; Van Maanen, 1983). Where ten years ago, the dominant metaphor for organization was the 'rational system,' today organizations are seen as 'garbage cans,' 'tribes,' or 'cultures.' When ten years ago, the only acceptable methodology for scholarly work was the quantified survey or experiment, today, some organizational scholars employ field work, conversation analysis, and rhetorical criticism.[1]

But as Geertz himself cautions, this opening up of disciplinary boundaries is not without peril. "If the result is not to be elaborate chatter or the higher nonsense, a critical consciousness will have to be developed."[2] The question then for a study like this one is - how do we know it to represent a useful blurring of genres rather than "elaborate chatter" or "the higher nonsense?" It is by locating the study in the stream of ongoing organizational research that we can begin to formulate an answer.

A useful starting point for locating this study is the frequently cited category scheme of Gibson Burrell and Gareth Morgan in their Sociological Paradigms and Organizational Analysis where they explicate four major paradigms of organizational analysis.

These four paradigms are articulated in terms of two different dimensions: the subjective-objective view of reality and the radical change-regulation aspect of social order. Subjectivists regard social reality as socially constructed, whereas objectivists view it as something operating external to the individual. Radical change theorists focus on social domination, conflict and change, whereas a regulation stance regards social stability and order as the building blocks of society.[3] From these two dimensions, then, four distinct paradigms emerge. Functionalists regard reality as objective and orderly. Interpretive theorists view reality as constituted in the subjective experiences of individuals and exhibit a concern for social order. Both radical humanists and radical structuralists maintain a critical stance in regard to social order, treating society as evolving through conflict, but radical humanists locate oppressive realities in the constructions of individuals, whereas radical structuralists locate them in forces outside the individual - capitalism, for example.

In this case study, the assumptions of the interpretive paradigm[4] are reflected. Rather than the experimental explication of objective phenomena, I am concerned with gaining an understanding of the experience of individuals. That is, my focus is on explaining subjective meaning rather than discovering causal laws. In addition, my emphasis is on regulation rather than radical change of the social order in the organization. That is, I stress an explication and understanding of the cohesive and unifying elements of organizational life rather than the elements of conflict and oppression. I am interested in understanding and interpreting organizational reality rather than critiquing it in terms of its effect on organizational members. In this case study, then, I am not concerned with organizational effectiveness, outcome, or change, but rather with understanding those organizational processes which provide a consensual social reality for organizational participants. This concern, then, is admittedly not within the mainstream of traditional organizational studies. Most organizational res earch follows the functionalist paradigm. Thus to provide a better understanding of the interpretive paradigm as I will use it, it may be useful to delineate the assumptions from which it operates, particularly those that differentiate it from a broad conception of the functionalist paradigm. Linda Putnam identifies some basic assumptions and articulates them in terms of similarities as well as differences between the two approaches.[5]

The first distinction between functionalist and interpretive approaches focuses on the nature of social reality. Functionalists treat social phenomenon as

concrete and materialistic - types of social facts.
Reality exists external to the individual and takes
form prior to any human activity.[6] Collectivities,
therefore, exist outside individuals, and their
properties, such as values, roles and norms, are
regarded as hard, tangible facts.[7]

An interpretive approach, however, reflects the
view of Peter Berger and Thomas Luckmann that reality
is socially constructed through the words, symbols, and
behavior of its members.[8] From this perspective
reality is defined, maintained and redefined in
communicative experience. Reality is not a place where
actions occur, nor does it determine actions. It
exists for organizational members only in its creation
by them. The ontological status of reality, outside
the experience of the individual, is regarded as
problematic. Burrell and Morgan contend that an
interpretive approach "rejects any view which
attributes to the social world a reality which is
independent of the minds of (people)."[9] From this
perspective, collectivities are "symbolic processes
that evolve through streams of ongoing behavior instead
of through static social facts."[10] Interpretive
researchers focus on the meanings attached to symbols
and the interactions that create and alter them.[11]

Putnam points out two additional assumptions
related to social reality. One deals with the
reification of structures and the other focuses on the
debate between volunteerism and determinism.

Reification involves the projection of the
characteristics of material substances onto symbolic
form. It is the act of transforming abstract, symbolic
forms into concrete, empirical facts.[12] According to
Putnam, both functionalists and interpretivists reify
structures, but the two paradigms differ in the way

they conceptualize structure. Functionalists reify structures by treating organizations as containers or entities and assuming social structures as existing prior to individual action.[13] They ignore the creation of structure by regarding individual action in terms of fixed properties.

Interpretivists, on the other hand, treat structures as "sets of complex, semiautonomous relationships that originate from human interactions."[14] Organizational members in daily action and interaction create structures, such as departments, levels and procedures that impinge on organizations and may run counter to existing structures.

For functionalists, then, structures are fixed and concrete and exist independently of the processes that create and change them. For interpretivists, however, structure and process are ongoing human activities, and structure is an outgrowth of sets of relationships that has real consequences on everyday interaction.[15]

These assumptions lead to two divergent views of organizing behavior. A functionalist perspective typically assumes a unitary view of organizations, in that they are regarded as cooperative systems in pursuit of common goals.[16] The organizational entity is the primary unit of analysis and its characteristics become static properties rather than social processes.[17] Interpretivists, however, are more likely to adopt a pluralistic view of organization.[18] Organizations are regarded as coalitions of participants with different priorities rather than monolithic entities. Individuals may subjugate their goals to the needs of the group, but they do not abandon them. They negotiate to achieve a common direction.[19]

Thus, in my case study the assumptions from which I am operating regard organizational reality as created and changed in interaction. This bookstore exists for organizational members in the meanings they assign to it. Furthermore, the ideology is reified in daily action and interaction and emerges in ongoing human activity as a structure that impinges on the day-to-day life of the organization. The organization, from this perspective, is made up of a diverse group of individuals negotiating to reach a shared understanding and achieve a common direction.

The functionalist and interpretive paradigms in organizational theory have come to be associated with different basic metaphors for organizations which theorists and researchers have developed as frameworks for analysis. The functionalist paradigm has been characterized by a reliance on the mechanistic metaphor of machine and the biological metaphor or organism.[20] The insights based on these two metaphors have formed the basis for orthodox organizational theory. The interpretive paradigm, on the other hand, has taken to using the metaphor of culture[21] to talk about organizational life.

An interpretive approach to organizational culture concentrates on coming to an understanding of the way organizational life is accomplished communicatively. The focus is on the networks of meanings as embodied in the language, rituals, stories of organizational members. Victor Turner regards these as essential to an understanding of how organizational realities are created and sustained.[22]

With the utilization of a cultural metaphor, the reseacher assumes a semiotic stance. Clifford Geertz, following Max Weber, regards cultures as "webs of significance" which are spun by cultural members in their day-to-day lives. The webs, or patterns of significant symbols, are conventionalized, consensual structures by which members orient themselves and make sense of their world.[23] The underlying presumption here is that symbols have arbitrary meaning and that organizational life is constituted by the process of defining, redefining and modifying those meanings.

An understanding of the organizational experience of individuals, how they makes sense of experiences, can be gained by an analysis of slices of that experience. Organizational reality, then, gains meaning only as it is defined in the experience of organizational members.[24] This study will focus on sense-making as it relates to the development and enactment of the ideology of organizational members as it is evident in the day-to-day life of the bookstore/coffeehouse.

In selecting ideology as a focus of this study, I have found Geertz's conception of ideology most useful.[25] Geertz regards ideology as a cultural model. It functions as a template or blueprint for the "organization of social and psychological processes, much as genetic systems provide such a template for the organization of organic processes."[26] Culture patterns (religious, philosophical, aesthetic, scientific, and ideological), says Geertz, are "programs." Whatever else ideologies may be - disguises for ulterior motives, phatic expressions of group solidarity, projections of unacknowledged fears - they are, Geertz says, most distinctly "maps of problematic social reality and matrices for the creation of collective conscience."[27] From Geertz's perspective, ideologies attempt to render "otherwise incomprehensible social situations meaningful, to so construe them as to make it possible to act purposefully within them."[28] This

focus on the constraining and enabling features of
culture's ideology seems most appropriate to this
study.[29]

What distinguishes Geertz's conception from others
and makes it most appropriate and useful here is that
inherent in his definition is the concept of symbolic
action. It is not enough to say that ideologies serve
functions in organizations, such as explaining action.
It is important to understand how they function to
mediate meanings, how they accomplish what it is they
do.

Rather than addressing the traditional questions
of the functionalist paradigm which regard ideology as
a variable which affects organizational outcome,
thinking in terms of symbolic action allows us to ask
questions about changes within the meanings assigned to
ideologies by organizational members. Within the realm
of meaning, ideologies are modified and redefined. It
is these changes in the way ideology works in terms of
individual and collective meanings assigned to them by
organizational members that is the focus of this study.
Rather than focusing on the dialectical tension between
the existing and competing ideologies, this perspective
focuses on the dialectical tension between what the
participants see themselves doing and their utopian
conception of the organization's ideology: between the
way things are and the way things ought to be. Crises
occur and are met in terms of movement toward a
continuously defined and redefined ideal.
Understanding the organization in terms of this
dialectical tension allows us to examine specific
ideological components, sisterhood for example, in
terms of a comparison between an ideal to which
organizational members are committed and the way the
ideology is enacted in day-to-day life. This is not to

say that these ideals or utopian conceptions are stable entities, only that they are regarded as meanings existing outside the enactment. These comparisons are made explicit in the talk and are the facilitators of organizational change as for example when one organizational member calls attention to the tensions between ideology and practice by announcing, "Hey, I don't think what we've been doing here is sisterhood. We need to make some changes."

My purpose is to examine this particular organization in terms of the interrelationship between ideology and action as it emerges in the interaction of organizational participants.[30] How, for example, is the ideological component of separatism enacted? How do the productions of separatism define, modify or sustain the concept and what is the relationship between ideological productions and organizational change?

This dissertation then, is located within those critical studies that aim to explain and understand human behavior rather than predict and alter it. It is, as Geertz says, "a matter of connecting action to its sense rather than behavior to its determinants."[31] Grounded in an interpretive approach to organizations, my perspective aims at a critical analysis of those cultural factors, in this case ideology, that can provide explanations of organizational reality. It utilizes those aspects of several interpretive approaches that best 'fit' with what it is I want to accomplish and represents the flexibility and variability of interpretive accounts of organizational life evident in the "interpretive turn"[32] in organizational studies today.

Feminist Ideology

Examining the ideology of this organization only
in terms of its enactment in the organization is
problematic because the feminist ideology evident there
does not exist in a vacuum. It is interactive with
feminist theory because organizational members read
theory and apply what they read to their enactment of
the business. Inasmuch as the ideology is based in and
interactive with feminist theory it therefore can be
regarded as part of the organizational text I have
constructed for analysis.

Feminism is most often thought of in terms of
action-oriented goals: equal pay for equal work, equal
representation in government, passage of the ERA: but
seldom is it regarded as a cohesive set of ideas which
provide a framework for action. In an assessment of
the state of feminist ideology, Judith Sabrosky
contends that this failure to develop as an
intellectual tradition can be blamed for the sporadic
treatment and diversity of ideas evident in feminist
theory. Contemporary feminists have been preoccupied,
she says, with goal achievement and have neglected the
study of feminist thought.[33]

Feminist theorists such as Sabrosky and Joanna
Russ, point to the absence of a cohesive body of
thought recongizable as a feminist ideology or
philosophy. Russ locates the reasons for this failure
in the traditional belief or concept of ideology which
equates it with internalized oppression. "Since open
force and economic coercion are practical only part of
the time, ideology - that is, internalized oppression,
the voice in the head - is brought in to fill the
gap."[34]

Due to this diversity in feminist thought, I have
elected to examine those ideological components which

emerge in the interaction and can be located in current feminist writings. The theoretical discussions of the concepts reflect the diversity of thought and are drawn from some popular literature as well as theoretical statements.

Methodology

In view of the assumptions of the interpretive approach, the methodological goal of this study is to gain access to the members' 'point of view' and to explicate those activities whereby members make their everyday experiences visibly reportable and accountable. Burrell and Morgan contend that this can only be accomplished by "occupying the frame of reference of the participant in action,"[35] by 'getting inside' situations and involving oneself in the everyday flow of life. Given this emphasis on the analysis of subjective experience, the most appropriate methodology for this study is participant observation. This choice enables the researcher to adopt a member's viewpoint and thereby gain an understanding of the collectivity's shared knowledge of 'what is going on.' The method calls for the researcher to participate in the interaction of the group under study on an ongoing basis and have some "nominal status for them as someone who is part of their daily lives."[36] That I achieved this nominal status was evident in the fact that I was invited to become a collective member and when I declined the offer was granted "honorary" status!

In engaging in participant observation, the researcher becomes immersed in the data to learn the actor's definition of the situation by thinking and acting as she does, seeing things as she sees them, participating in the actor's reality and then distancing herself from the data, transcending the

experience, permitting her to see what the actor does
not and to analyze it for patterns, process and common
denominators.[37]

Field research has traditionally been carried out
by an outsider or stranger who enters a cultural
situation and attempts to understand and interpret it.
There is, however, another vantage point from which
research can be conducted - that of the insider,[38] the
individual who is a member of the group under study.
In this particular research effort, the problem of
access necessitated an insider stance. In all field
research, practical considerations such as the
fieldworker's age, ethnic identity, or gender can
prevent access to the community or severly limit the
knowledge to which the researcher has access.[39] The
matter of trust is crucial. An outsider is often the
subject of suspicion when conducting research among a
minority population.[40] This is particularly true in the
group under study. In this study, my gender identity
gained me access to an environment closed to most
researchers, and I was able to operate in the setting
as an overt observer.

As a participant observer, I attended business
meetings and social organizational functions and was
considered an 'honorary,' nonvoting member of the
collective. Occasionally, I assisted in maintaining
the kitchen, making sandwiches and waiting on
customers. Often I helped customers in the bookstore
or answered the phone. I achieved 'membership' status
by being included in the activities of the collective.
In effect, I became an insider in the organization.

This 'insider' status was thus essential inasmuch as an outsider would be regarded with suspicion and never permitted the access to information and interaction that I, as a community member and honorary collective member, was afforded. It was also essential because much of the decision making and discussion that goes on occurs in a social rather than business setting, and even the business meetings are intense with personal issues often being discussed.

Conclusion

I take Geertz's challenge, to develop a critical consciousness so that the blurring of genres does not result in "elaborate chatter of the higher nonsense," to be the taking off point for this study. With that in mind, I have in this chapter, located my study in terms of the theoretical perspective and intellectual traditions in which it is grounded; in terms of the social-historical context in which it is situated; and in terms of the methodologogy I used in approaching it. But perhaps the usefulness of the approach is not so much in its location in a body of scholarly thought, or in a social-historical context, but in "the story it allows me to tell."[41]

CHAPTER 1
NOTES

[1]Mary S. Strine and Michael Pacanowsky, "How to Read
Interpretive Accounts of Organizational Life: The
'Positionality' of the Researcher as an Informing
Principle," unpublished manuscript, University of Utah,
1984, p. 2.

[2]Clifford Geertz, "Blurred Genres: The Refiguration of
Social Thought," American Scholar (Spring 1980) p. 168.

[3]Gibson Burrell and Gareth Morgan, Sociological
Paradigms and Organizational Analysis (London:
Heinemann, 1979).

[4]Linda Putnam, "Paradigms for Organizational Communication Research: An Overview and Synthesis," Western
Journal of Speech Communication, Vol. 46, No. 2, Spring
1982, p. 200.

An interpretive approach is actually a generic
approach which is made up of four major schools of
thought: hermeneutics, symbolic interactionism, ethnomethodology and phenomenology. It is, however, a
paradigm with a common core in the centrality of
meaning in social actions. The roots of these approaches can be found in German idealism, particularly
in Immanuel Kant's belief that social reality exists in
"spirit or idea" rather than in concrete social facts.
Specifically, interpretive approaches aim to explicate
the subjective and consensual meanings that constitute
social reality.

Actually, each of these schools is comprised of a
number of diverse subgroups. Like the interpretive
paradigm there is an eclectic nature to the approach
adopted for this study. I locate my work within this
paradigm with the recognition that an organizational
culture approach does not fit squarely within one of
these major schools, but rather is grounded in concepts
characteristic of three of them.

From hermeneutic theorists (Ricoeur, 1982), for
example, I have adopted the metaphor of text, casting
social experiences into a symbolic document that is
read and translated in terms of patterns, themes and

symbolic processes. The approach is concerned with the
way "in which the structure of discourse may explore
certain key themes and develop particular kinds of
imagery." (Gareth Morgan, 1980) Within organizational
studies, Susan Koch and Stanley Deetz's (1981) metaphorical analysis of a university news service department
and Anne Huff's examination on arguments as organizational documents, exemplify the hermeneutic perspective.

An emphasis on the creation of shared meanings
through symbolic behavior, in this study on the ways in
which organizational members construct a shared
understanding of the organization's ideology, is
characteristic of a symbolic interaction perspective.
Examples of this perspective in organizational study
are Meryl Reis Louis' (1980) work on organizational
socialization and Linda Harris and Vernon E. Cronen's
rule-based model of organizational communication.

Much research conducted within the interpretive
paradigm adopts some variation of ethnomethodology
(Garfinkel, 1979), the study of how people construct
common sense knowledge. Conversational analysis and
examinations of enacted culture, two topics focused on
by ethnomethodologists, are evident in my study.

[5]Linda Putnam, "The Interpretive Perspective: An
Alternative to Functionalism," Communication and
Organizations: An Interpretive Approach, Linda Putnam
and Michael Pacanowsky, ed. (Beverly Hills: Sage
Publications, Inc., 1983), pp. 31-54.

[6]G. Ritzer, "Sociology: A Multiple Paradigm Science,"
American Sociologist, 10 (1975), 156-167.

[7]G. Ritzer, p. 162.

[8]Peter Berger and Thomas Luckman, The Social Construction of Reality (Garden City, New Jersey: Doubleday
and Co., Inc., 1966).

[9]Gibson Burrell and Gareth Morgan, p. 10.

[10]G. Ritzer, p. 164.

[11]G. Ritzer, p. 164.

[12]D. L. Swenson, "On the Use of Symbolist Insight in
the Study of Political Communication," Human Communica-

tion Research, No. 8, 1982, pp. 379-382.

[13]M. Zey-Farrell and M. Aiken, "Introduction to
Critiques of Dominant Perspectives," Complex Organizations: Critical Perspectives, M. ZeyFarrell and M.
Aiken, eds. (Glenview: Illinois: Scott, Foresman,
1981).

[14]Linda Putnam, 1983, p. 35.

[15]Linda Putnam, 1983, p. 35.

[16]Gibson Burrell and Gareth Morgan

[17]M. Zey-Farrell and M. Aiken

[18]Linda Putnam, 1983, p. 37.

[19]Karl E. Weick, "Organizational Communication: Toward
a Research Agenda," in Communication and Organizations:
An Interpretive Approach, Linda Putnam and Michael
Pacanowsky, eds. (Beverly Hills: Sage Publications,
1983).

[20]Gareth Morgan, "Paradigms, Metaphors and Puzzle
Solving in Organization Theory," Administrative Science
Quarterly, Vol. 25, No. 4, Dec. 1980, pp. 605-622.

Gareth Morgan (1980) suggests that the field has
been imprisoned by these metaphors and that the
metaphors of other paradigms which challenge the
assumptions of functionalist metaphors may create "new
ways of viewing organizations which overcome the
weaknesses and blindspots of traditional metaphors,
offering supplementary or even contradictory approaches
to organizations." It is not that one metaphor can be
regarded as better than others, but that different
metaphors can capture and constitute the nature of
organizational life in different ways, providing unique
but necessarily partial insights.

[21]Gareth Morgan, p. 610.

Morgan points out that the interpretive metaphor of
culture can be used in a functionalist manner. To use
the metaphor this way necessitates regarding culture as
something an organization has. According to Michael
Pacanowsky and Nick O'Donnell-Trujillo (1984), this
functionalist orientation trivializes the metaphor,
reducing it to just another variable to be located in

the organization and measured in terms of organizational effectiveness.

[22]Victor Turner, "Foreward" in Number Our Days Barbara
Myerhoff, (New York: Simon and Schuster, 1978).

[23]Clifford Geertz, The Interpretation of Cultures (New
York: Basic Books, 1973).

[24]To come to an understanding of an organization's
culture and to make sense of an organization's sense-
making, some researchers focus on indicators or
displayers of that sense-making. Pacanowsky and
O'Donnell-Trujillo identify these as the rites and
rituals of organizational life, the relevant constructs
and social facts used by organizational members to
explain the organization, and the vocabulary, metaphors, and stories of organizational participants.
Borman (1983) focuses on the dynamic sharing of group
fantasies. Deal and Kennedy (1982) suggest studying
the organization's heroes, rites and rituals, values,
and cultural network.

[25]Another useful idea is the conception of ideology
presented by J. S. Roucek in A History of the Concept
of Ideology (1976): "strictly a system of ideas
elaborated in the light of certain conceptions of what
'ought to be.' It designates a theory of social life
which approaches facts from the point of view of an
ideal, and interprets them, consciously or unconscious-
ly, to prove the correctness of its analysis and to
justify that ideal."

[26]Clifford Geertz, "Ideology as a Cultural System," in
Ideology and Discontent, David Apter, ed. (London:
Collier McMillan, Ltd., 1964).

[27]Clifford Geertz, 1964, p. 64.

[28]Clifford Geertz, 1964, p. 64.

[29]Traditional organizational studies have focused
primarily on the constraining features of ideologies.
Roger Dunbar (1982) sees ideologies as instruments of
stagnation, Nils Brunsson (1982) sees them as retro-
spective justifications for irrational decision-making.
Although William Starbuck (1982) sees ideologies as
concepts invented to meet crisis situations, an
alternative definition is provided by Alan Meyer (1982)
who contends that organizational ideologies "legitimate

certain actions, render other actions heretical, evoke historical reinterpretations and create meanings for events that have yet to occur."

[30]The benefit in examining the dialectical tension between the ideology and action is pointed to by Karl Weick (1983) in his explication of a research agenda for the field of organizational communication. He applies the principle that "every datum becomes meaningful only when there is a relatum" to studies which examine talk as a means of understanding what is going on in an organization as if the talk itself stands alone and 'means something." Talk, Weick contends, is worth little without comparison, even though it has a way of seeming obvious, sufficient, and inevitable. "In their zeal to show how much can be done with small snatches of talk, conversational analysts have overlooked the fact that things make sense only when they are put alongside something else." In this study, the specific ideological components and the organization provide that 'something else' to which talk can be compared.

[31]Clifford Geertz, 1965, p. 178.

[32]Michael Pacanowsky and Mary Strine, p. 2.

[33]Judith Sabrosky, p. 148.

[34]Joanna Russ, "Power and Helplessness in the Women's Movement," in Sinister Wisdon, No. 18, Fall 1981.

[35]Gibson Burrell and Gareth Morgan.

[36]Maxine Bacca Zinn, "Field Research in Minority Communities: Ethical, Methodological and Political Observations by an Insider," Social Problems, Vol. 27, No. 2, December 1979, p. 211.

[37]James A. Anderson, "Teaching Qualitative Methods," A paper presented at the AEJ Convention, Athens, Ohio, 1982, p. 5.

[38]Whether research can be more fruitfully conducted by an outsider or an insider is a major methodological issue in discussions of participant observation. The argument basically involves the contention that the insider's proximity to the data precludes her ability to remain objective. On the other hand, those who advocate an insider stance maintain that the insider is

"endowed with special insight into matters necessarily obscure to others, thus possessed of a penetrating discernment." Howard Schwartz and Jerry Jacobs, Qualitative Sociology: A Method to the Madness (New York: Macmillan, 1979), p. 46.

[39]There is a growing literature on the effects of gender and sex in field research. An example of this can be found in Warren's (1974) research on the secret gay male world. Her gender prevented her gaining access to entire areas of the gay world used by men: baths, tearooms and cliques of men hostile to women. The result was a focus on sociability almost to the exclusion of sexuality.

[40]Maxine Bacca Zinn, p. 209.

[41]Michael Pacanowsky and Nick O'Donnell-Trujillo, p. 29.

CHAPTER II

THE ORGANIZATIONAL FOCUS

This chapter is concerned with three major contextual factors of this study. Specifically, it discusses 1) the concept of feminist business, including an explication of a collective business structure and an examination of the women's bookstore network, 2) the four major developmental stages of the business under study, Twenty Rue Jacob, and it provides 3) an ethnographic description of the business setting and clientele.

These three areas are vital to an understanding of the ideology and its relationship to the organization. The position of ideology in feminist business is unique because the business emerges as an ideological effort and can be regarded as an enactment of that ideology. Therefore, the development of the ideological components and the structure of the business and the business setting, as well as the interaction of the organizational members, can be regarded as productions of ideology and are therefore an integral part of the analysis.

The Concept of Feminist Business

With the resurgence of the women's movement in the 1970s, women's businesses began to emerge both as an alternative work environment for women and as a means of gaining economic power and independence. Women's record companies, publishing firms, bookstores and coffeehouses were established with the ultimate aim of providing a network through which women could market their talents and products, opportunities which women felt they had often been denied through traditional patriarchal organizations. Women's businesses were there to provide opportunities which otherwise would not exist. Thus the feminist business is, as an organization, a unique ideological and cultural product.

Feminists[1] regard male-dominated business and industry as a political entity. Within male-created and dominate structures (business, organization or professions) women are in the minority and isolated from one another. They are victimized by male hierarchical structures, the basic assumption being that they cannot work within a system they did not create and within which they have no power. Even if their day-to-day commitment is to their colleagues and their workplace, "the ultimate commitment of women who want to advance the cause of women must be to other competent, able women."[2] This basic feminist concept of sisterhood is not a creation of modern women who have only recently been accorded the status that enables them to operate in the male-dominated world of work. As early as 1840 Margaret Fuller advocated that rather than joining with men "women should themselves take up weapons and mutually help each other."[3] The concept of feminist business is regarded as a political response to male-dominated business.

It is out of this notion that the concept and definition of feminist business emerges. Feminist writers make a clear distinction here between the process and the product. A feminist business is not necessarily one which sells feminist-oriented products. Hannah Darby and Brooke Williams point out that the "products do not affect the nature of the business as such. . ."[4] The nature of the business, Jennifer Woodul claims, "will be changed by the feminist operation of it."[5] Incorporated into the idea of a different process is the adherence to different goals -- the feminist organization is any organization in which policy and finances are controlled by women who are feminist in orientation and in which the basic goal of the organization is to provide an environment where "work is done that in one way or another builds and strengthens the women's movement and leads toward fundamental change in our society."[6]

A business exists and to some extent is dependent on a community's needs for its products to survive. As a business in this society, any feminist business must work within a capitalistic framework to succeed. For this reason many feminist theorists regard the concept of feminist business as problematic. Darby and Williams, for example, contend that feminist business is contradictory. Capitalism and feminism, they argue, are antithetical because capitalism is a patriarchal framework.[7] It is even regarded by some as an advanced stage of patriarchy. Feminist business, at some point, will not work without compromising the ideology. For this reason many feminist businesses experiment with alternative structures, such as a collective system which emphasizes relationship and worker satisfaction

as opposed to profit. Even so, many postulate that
feminist businesses simply create a new market which
can be exploited by male-dominated industries, which
because of their relative strength will economically
ruin feminist business.

Despite these controversies, other feminists
believe it is time to claim economic power. Many of
these women still have reservations as to whether
capitalism and feminism can mix successfully, but they
believe that since "it is not yet within our scope to
do away with an oppressive system" women must use the
basics of the system to their own advantage.[8] Politically aware women, they contend, will not buy 'feminist' products[9] created by male-dominated industry
inasmuch as spending money with women-oriented business
has become a political commitment. Given these
assumptions, a feminist business is essentially a
political organization committed to radical political
and economic changes in society, which is willing to
recognize current political and economic realities in
order to get power for women right now.

Woodul, of Olivia Records, echoes the necessity of
getting on with it now. "There must be a commitment to
radical change--to the goals of economic and political
power for women."[10] That is, feminist businesses, by
their very existence, can play an active role in
espousing these goals. They can assist in formulating
and attaining them. They are regarded as models for
the future. As Jo Freeman and Carol Macmillan note,
"We are a young movement and do not have a totally
clear theory and direction. . . this will grow in part
from an examination of the organization we are building. Work in the feminist organization serves as a
base for further developing our political ideas."[11]

Woodul regards feminist businesses as the wave of the future. They are designed by women to meet the needs of women and to become what we want them to become. "They are superb inventions which test our feminist principles in crises of the everyday decisions which are momentous because they have everything to do with our survival-- politically and economically."[12]

From a feminist perspective, then, a feminist business formulated and operated by women is an enactment of feminist ideology. At the core of their purpose is the process of finding ways in the day-today working of the business to achieve the goals of economic and political power for women. "Without feminist organizations, feminism is limited to an abstract concept. At our workplaces it becomes a living reality."[13]

Inasmuch as feminist organizations exist for their ideology, they provide a rich opportunity for examining the enactment of ideology in organizations and for analyzing the relationship between that ideology and organizational change.

Collectivism as a Feminist Organizational Model

For the feminist theorist, the concept of collec-tivism is a vital one. In feminist ideology, a collective serves as a social change model and as such provides a workplace structure and environment consis-tent with feminist ideals. For this reason, many feminist businesses operate as a collective[14] or at least experiment with the form for a period of time.

There are two reasons why the collective structure has such an appeal to feminist thinking. First, the principle of consensus in decision-making is egalitar-ian and is a denial of traditional hierarchical

structure. Collectives by definition want all workers
to have equal input into the running of the group.
Second, the collective system enables women, who
individually lack the capital and/or training to begin
a business, to do so as a group, sharing the leadership, the work and the financial burden.

The key word for the feminists in the collective
system is 'empowerment.'[15] That is, the system focuses
on giving power to control individual direction.
Collectives provide an alternative work environment in
that the emphasis is on the individual rather than the
group. Thus, relationship takes precedence over
profit; new forms of work provide models for new styles
of relationships, rather than being regarded as new
means of increasing production.

A collective system, however, cannot be regarded as
an instrument for replacing capitalism, but only as a
very limited alternative to it. Karen Brandow, in No
Bosses Here, writes that many social change theorists
are critical of collective systems because, while they
can be regarded as successful alternative work models,
they cannot be seen as enough in themselves to bring
about social change.[16] The major reason for this,
Brandow says, is since collectives are limited to
operating in a capitalist society, they cannot be
regarded as a viable means of producing new wealth.

Paula Griese, in her analysis of food cooperatives
notes that you cannot make a revolution merely by
existing and growing. "It is not possible to build an
alternative society quietly and peacefully, wholly
outside the mainstream society, for the latter's rules
control most of the wealth and means of producing new
wealth.... If an alternative looks likely to threaten
this (the status quo), they fight it. If you cannot

defend your 'alternative,' they win."[17]

Despite this limitation in terms of social change, collectives are regarded as a powerful model for alternative work environments. "Any movement for fundamental change in this country will only succeed if it offers a model of what we are working for, and a consistent way of working for it. This is the contribution of collectives."[18] A collective structure, then, cannot be considered a means of accumulating wealth for women or an instrument for changing the patriarchal structure of society, but it can be regarded as a powerful model for the enactment of feminist principles in the individual workplace.

According to Brandow, feminist collectives make up a large part of the collective movement. They provide women an opportunity to pool their resources and regain control over important aspects of their lives. Many women choose to work in all-women groups to "develop new feminist approaches to problems."[19] But the primary impetus, from a radical feminist perspective, is to provide a challenge to the traditional hierarchical nature of organizations, which is regarded as patriarchal and a means for continuing the oppression of women.

The business under study operated as a collective for approximately one year during 1982 and 1983. At a collective meeting, one member talked about the relevance of the structure for the women of Twenty Rue Jacob:

> Getting into this kind of business
> venture, it was an alternative to working in
> a traditional system that was seen as
> oppressive and we wanted an alternative
> feminist-type business to be part of.[20]

During the time that this business functioned as a collective, the ideological benefits such as providing an alternative work space, challenging hierarchical structure, providing a laboratory for feminist principles, were evident in the interaction of organizational members. These benefits were talked about and acted on. Equality was an expectation, regardless of status, and the focus was on the sharing of responsibility, work and reward. Many of the tensions within the structure, and in fact, the failure of the collective form in this organization, may be attributed to this expectation.

But, in spite of the fact that many incoming collective members regarded the alternative structure as a reason for becoming involved, it was not the reason for the formation of the collective in the first place. The need was for more money and more workers and the collective was the most practical way of solving the business problems.

Collective systems in individual feminist enterprises exist within a wider context. In the case of this bookstore coffeehouse, that wider context is a women's bookstore network.

The Women's Bookstore Network

Women's bookstores began to appear on the scene in the early 1970s with the resurgence of interest in women's subjects and the establishment of the feminist presses. Early business efforts ranged from volunteer-staffed, one-room stores to tables set up at conferences, in women's buildings or resource centers and on university campuses.

Today, there are approximately 80-110 such stores in the United States, most small, but many mature

stable businesses.[21] The network system that connects
them is a publication, The Feminist Bookstore News,
edited and published by Carol Seajay, a founder and
former owner of the San Francisco bookstore, Old Wives'
Tales. The bimonthly publication, which links bookstore owners and publishers, was established in 1976 at
a Women in Print Conference.

A Ms. magazine assessment of the women's bookstore
network notes that each bookstore has an individual
style which is reflected in its offerings. Some, such
as Twenty Rue Jacob, the focus of this study, special-
ize in lesbian books and women's art work. Others,
such as Charis Books and More in Atlanta, carry books
by both men and women in a wide range of areas. "We
want to suggest that feminism is a world view," says
Charis owner, Kay Hogan, "that looks at everything -
from birth control and wife-battering to appropriate
technology and holistic health."[22]

Some stores combine bookselling with a coffeehouse
effort, such as Artemis in San Francisco, Bloodroot in
Bridgeport, Connecticut and Twenty Rue Jacob in Salt
Lake City. But, despite the diversity in offerings,
almost all serve as a community clearinghouse, referral
service and a social center, and most often this is
conceived of as the major function of the bookstore.
However, as the enactment of feminist principles and
the model of a "yet to come" matriarchy, feminist
businesses are regarded by organizational members as
political as well as social entities.

Jeanne O'Connor, in her Ms. article, states that
"almost every women's bookseller will say that her
motivation for starting the store was political, rather
than financial."[23] Alex, owner of Twenty Rue Jacob
often jokes with customers, "What, do you think I'm in

this to make money?" The reality of it is, she says, that "you don't do this to get rich, but it would be nice."[24] In this respect, it is often the ideology more than the promise of financial gain that is the major organizing factor for the business. That is, the intent is to serve as an active force in building a separate women's culture and it is hoped, a new society.

Ideology also often figures heavily in the maintenance of the feminist bookstore in terms of conflict or financial problems. The 1982-83 struggle for control of A Woman's Place bookstore in San Francisco is an illustrative example. A major conflict and legal battle began when the founder and original store owner and one collective member locked out the four other collective members due to business and personal disagreements. Ideological concerns figure heavily in the decision handed down by the three female arbitrators. The decision was made to stabilize and maintain the business while at the same time phasing out the current collective owners. This decision to maintain rather than dissolve the business was based on the agreement of all parties "that their primary concern (was) the survival of the bookstore as an asset of the women's community." The first point in the body of the decision states "1. ICI - A Woman's Place bookstore is a political business formed for the benefit of the women's community, the essence of which is decision-making by unanimous agreement, i.e. consensus."[25] Thus, the ideology of the feminist bookstore is instrumental in both the formation, and the continuation, of these feminist organizations.

To facilitate an understanding of the way ideology is enacted in the creation and maintenance of Twenty

Rue Jacob, a detailed account of its creation and
development is essential. This history is organized
around four basic shifts representing four stages of
development in this business. 1) The creation stage
details the individual and social needs out of which
the business emerged. 2) The initial three-owner
partnership stage served as a time of definition and
direction. 3) The collective stage was experimental in
that responsibility was divided among the twelve
business owners and a redefinition of the business
occurred. 4) A three-owner partnership stage followed
the failure of the collective system.

The Creation Stage

Among organizational members there is a general
belief that lesbians experience a sense of social
isolation at least at some point in their lives. This
is most often said to occur when they are discovering
their lesbian identity and 'coming out,'[26] when they
emerge from a long-term isolated or dependent relationship, or when they move to a new community. There is
an overwhelming need to establish and maintain a
community within which the individual feels a sense of
belonging. Potential friends are chosen and evaluated
in terms of their community membership. 'The community' is personified and it is generally believed
that portions of that community will emerge at certain
places (bookstores, bars) or certain events (women's
conferences, concerts, etc.).

Traditionally, lesbians regard the local women's
bar as the most obvious and often the only place to get
in touch with the community in most cities. For many
women who cannot feel comfortable in such an environment, or those who are trying to maintain some secrecy

in their lives, this alternative is not available.
Particularly for those women going through the emotional transition of 'coming out,' this particular setting
is regarded as frightening or threatening. In addition, only a small segment of the community, often very
young working class women, patronize the bars. For
lesbians, locating and identifying their community is a
continual process and often involves years of building
a network of friends and contacts. Organizational
members regard a bookstore as a nonthreatening,
homogeneous environment, which can provide access to
the wider community for many who would otherwise have
only limited social connections. As Alex recounted in
her account of the bookstore's creation, it was out of
this need to alleviate a sense of social isolation and
identify a 'community' that Twenty Rue Jacob came into
existence.

In 1978 she was living in Salt Lake City and
feeling very alone.[27] Although she was living with
another woman, she reported feeling a need to identify
herself with a community of women with a similar
lifestyle. She began ordering books through the mail
which provided the kinds of information she was unable
to obtain through local bookstores. Among these were
books and records which were lesbian in orientation.

When I would buy a woman's album or a
lesbian-feminist album, the first thing I
would do even before I would put it on the
phonograph was I would take the album out of
the jacket and I would look at the insert
wrapper, because they always had pictures of
women and stories and the words to the songs,
and that was real important to me - it was

> kind of my contact with the outer world. Um,
> I was really closeted, I had no resources
> with which to fill my (social needs). . .[28]

She had been ordering heavily from feminist publishers and buying feminist books from traditional publishing houses and paying full price for them when she realized that perhaps she could find a more economical way to obtain her materials. She investigated the possibility of a business license, paid a $15 fee at the county courthouse and received a business license in the mail a few weeks later. She began putting her business license on her orders and requesting books at wholesale and publishers began sending her orders as a business.

As friends began to order through Alex books unavailable locally she found that the book ordering was demanding too much of her time. She invited two co-workers, both heterosexual women, to form a mail order book business with her and they set up shop in Alex's apartment. They named the business Hon Enterprises, a bilingual play on words as 'hon' means 'book' in Japanese. Their initial focus was on nonsexist children's literature, and feminist and bilingual books were very difficult to obtain locally.

The three partners, each of whom had initially put $50 into the account, compiled a mailing list and a sample sheet detailing the kinds of books available, purchased an answering machine to take orders while they were at work and sent out a mailing. The response was very encouraging.

Over the next year the business grew and was very steady, but never got to the point it could support anyone. In addition, Carol decided to drop out because she was taking too much time from her family. Alex and her other partner, Katie, continued to operate out of Alex's apartment.

The types of orders coming in slowly changed until at the end of the first year the focus was on feminist, lesbian and gay books.

> In the beginning, like I mentioned
> before, we had those kinda books that men
> ordered and we kinda went through a phase
> where a lotta children's books were being
> ordered, ya know we didn't know who these
> people were, and what happened was that
> people started ordering lesbian and feminist
> books (pause) and it was pretty unique.[29]

Because the nature of the business was changing and Alex found herself concentrating more and more on lesbian and feminist publishers, Katie decided it was time for her to leave and concentrate on other things. Alex struggled on with the business for several months alone.

In 1979 Alex met a group of women who were active in the lesbian community and was invited by two of them, Beth and Carolyn, to attend the Michigan Women's Music Festival.[30] It was this event that ultimately led to the restructure of the business to a walk-in bookstore/coffeehouse.

> We became so close and so loving and so
> complete and during the festival, the work-
> shops and the music and the witchcraft and
> all the wonderful things that music festivals
> bring to women. It was so intense and so

immense. I'll never forget getting out of
that car and looking at 10,000 women. Every
single one of them was a lesbian just like me
and they came from all walks of life and they
were poor and they were rich and they were
old and young and they were every color under
the sun and I actually saw third world women
and women of color. I actually spoke with
them and I actually made contact with them
and I wasn't the only one and it was beautiful.[31]

On the return to Salt Lake City, Alex and Beth and
Carolyn discussed the problems Alex was having keeping
her small mail order business going. She was ready to
close down and revert to ordering books for herself.

It was the first time that I realized
that maybe I was an asset to the lesbian
community. . . and I started thinking about
that and the more I thought about it the more
I talked about it, the more we talked about
it, the more it became a dream and the dream
became a reality and by the time we got to
Salt Lake City we had decided to take Hon
Enterprises and open it up as a walk-in
business.[32]

During the winter of 1980 the three found a
building and began getting it in shape to open. They
discussed names, like The Lavender Menace, The Purple
Parrot, The Iris and finally settled on Twenty Rue
Jacob.[33]
Preparing for an opening and renovating the

building in the winter presented a number of problems.
The exterior of the building needed painting, the roof
and the interior needed a lot of work, but the first
few weeks the building had no heat and it was a bad
winter.

> It had been snowing for weeks.
> Let's see, I remember, it was February
> 12, 1980, a Saturday morning. I woke up
> ready to bundle up real warm. I knew
> that the paint was going to be hard to
> paint on. . . The goddess had smiled on
> us and had given us a day that was the
> most incredible day in February.[34]

Beth and Carolyn had mentioned the painting day to
a couple of friends, but none of them anticipated the
response of the community. It confirmed their feelings
that the business would fulfill a need in the community.

> I got to the Rue and took out the paint
> brushes and paint and rollers and rags and
> these women started showing up. Women I had
> never seen before. . . and they had paint
> clothes on and rollers and brushes and rags
> and hats and said, 'Where do you want us to
> start?' They had ladders and more than
> anything else they had hope and in about six
> hours we had painted the complete outside of
> the building. We learned each others names.
> We shared with each other. About noon (we)
> went and bought more Kentucky Fried Chicken
> than I've ever seen in my life and a lot of

> beer and we sat and we ate together and we
> talked about what we wanted the Rue to be,
> about how we wanted people to feel comfort-
> able at the Rue and it was wonderful and the
> paint dried and then it snowed like hell for
> the rest of the winter.[35]

The recognition of this need on an individual level and
then on a community level prompted the formation of
first, a mail order book business, and then a walk-in
bookstore/coffeehouse.

The Initial Three-Owner Partnership

Over one hundred women came to the official opening
on February 27, 1980. Food was served and pictures
were taken to document the event. Many of the most
prominent members of the lesbian community showed up.

The weeks prior to the official opening were filled
with building bookshelves and renovating the interior.
Customers stopped in to visit or help, but mostly Alex
was alone.

> We didn't have heat the first few weeks
> and it was February. I'd take my guitar down
> and I'd make shelves or paint and then I'd go
> to 7-11 to warm up awhile. All in all it was
> an exhilarating time.[36]

Those first few weeks have become a part of organizational folklore. Stories are told, both by owners and
regular patrons of the days when Alex would "spend late
into the night sitting on the floor playing her
guitar."[37]

The first months were a time of defining the

business and determining direction. Initially the
bookstore had a limited stock of lesbian and feminist
books and little more than coffee was available in the
coffeehouse. Many of the regular customers were
friends of Carolyn and Beth. There was a lot of
uncertainty as to who the customers would be.

It was also more than a time for definition from
within. It was also a time for being defined by the
community at large. Alex reports that once several
women came in laughing and explained that several
children from across the street had yelled at them and
called them "faggots." "They didn't care so much about
being called names, but they wanted it to be correct."[38]

The vice squad started coming in and thumbing
through the books. Alex said they were distinguishable
because they were always dressed in a raincoat and had
short crew cut type hair styles. She told me of one
time a man and woman came in and looked through the
books. Alex was behind the counter in the bookstore
doing some paperwork when she noticed that the woman
was standing just behind the man, both with their backs
to her. The woman was holding something in her hand
behind her back that looked like an official ID and she
was holding it open. At first Alex did not think much
of it, but when the man started to turn, the woman
snapped it closed and buried it in her hand. "It was
as if she was trying to warn us."[39]

In spite of the seventy hours Alex was putting in
each week and the fact that the bookstore was open in
the evenings, business the first year was not good.
Payments were behind. The owners managed to hold
together for the first six months but by August the
situation was serious. They decided to hold out for a

few more months. "There were days then that I spent
all day there and took in no money."[40] When Christmas
came, business increased and the decision was made to
stick with it for another year.

In 1981, Beth and Alex were left to run the
business alone. Carolyn had met someone who was being
transferred to South Dakota and she chose to leave with
her. She wanted to sell her partnership for her
initial investment of $1500, but the problem was that
what was needed was a worker and most women with that
amount of money to invest did not have the time to also
work the business. Beth was tired, she had a son to
take care of and felt that the business was taking all
of her off-work time. The two made a decision to
close. An announcement was made to the community
through the Women Aware newsletter.[41] The response to
the announcement was panic. "You can't just close" was
the standard reaction. Beth and Alex reevaluated their
decision.

The Collective

The solution to the dilemma occurred to Alex as
she was investigating the structure of other bookstores. What she finally decided was that each
partnership should be divided into three. The result
was the formation of a nine-member collective. Carolyn
sold her three shares for $400 each and Alex and Beth
each sold two of their shares. Some of the shares were
owned jointly by two people, but had only one vote.
The collective, it was felt, would provide more input
and solve the work burden. The input was important in
the sense that it was felt that the customers were
still being defined. It was difficult for one person
to be sensitive to the needs of all the different

groups of women who were potential customers. "There was the bar group, the radical feminists, the professional women, the working class women and there was diversity in the collective, too."[42]

There is no provision for collectives in Utah law, so the business, from an official standpoint, became a partnership of nine (with three of the shares being owned jointly by two women each). Seven of nine votes were needed to make decisions, but according to Alex and as is evident in most of the collective meetings I attended during that time, this was seldom an issue. There was almost always a consensus on decisions.

The collective stage has been characterized as an experiment stage. Each collective member was committed to an agreed amount of participation, based on their commitments outside the business and the needs of other collective members. Almost all members were required to put in about six hours of work in the business each week, waiting on customers and serving food in the coffeehouse. Some members put in considerably more time than required during periods of unemployment or when they took work vacation. Others stretched it to the limits and barely put in the minimum.

Business meetings were referred to as collective meetings and retreats were planned periodically, either in the form of an all-day seminar-type situation or a planned overnight stay at a cabin or home. The retreats differed from the business meeting in that one member, who was a therapist, often facilitated sessions in which interpersonal issues were dealt with. Both personal and business decisions and directions were determined.

Membership in the collective was determined primarily by political and philosophical similarity.

While there was a financial commitment, it was negotiable in terms of a payment schedule. The involvement commitment was for one year.

The first collective member to leave made a decision to sell her membership to another woman eight months after the collective was initially formed. The new member attended a business meeting, was approved by the group and then purchased the share from the original woman. She remained as one of the last three owners.

The second collective member left shortly thereafter and returned her share to the business. The third share owned by two women was returned to the business about a month later. The major issue for all of these women was "burnout." People were tired of putting in the time and receiving "no return on their investment."

The initial feeling was that the collective had been too diversified and that a decrease in the number of collective members would be an improvement. Those active in the collective felt a need to weed out those who were unable to spend time at the business, who were only peripherally involved. This manifested itself at collective meetings in the beginning of the summer of 1983. No one was sure whether the business would hold up or not. Beth was no longer involved. Alex had taken a leave of absence, a "sabbatical," because she had spent all her energies for the first two years on the business and she needed some distance to re-group. The general feeling however was that the collective would continue on, smaller, stronger and more cohesive than before. The first move was to determine who would leave and who would commit to another year before the scheduled retreat in June. The second priority was to remaining members (a couple with a single share) made a decision to leave. They felt the amount of commitment needed to continue at their present level of involvement would seriously stunt their growth in other areas. One was anticipating beginning a Ph.D. program within the year and was finishing an M.A. program. She had figured prominently in the day-to-day running of the business and had taken on a strong leadership role in the business. They announced they would continue until August.

This left Alex and three collective members to run the business. All three of these women were able to devote only minimal time to the business. One had ceased involvement some time before and continued only with her financial obligation, another had accepted a job which involved frequent travel and was rarely available to work at all, and the third was able to work only on her days off. Alex was currently unemployed, but appeared emotionally unable and unwilling to make a commitment to return to the business full-time. Fortunately, the part-time employee hired earlier was able to cover those days when neither Alex nor Laurie could cover. The remaining members took some time to make up their minds. They seemed reluctant to drop out, but two felt they had no option.

Meanwhile, Alex was making a decision to close. She decided to file for bankruptcy because of the debts. Even if the three remaining decided to stay, the financial situation was bleak. The collective had returned the business to her and she was left with the decision. She decided to keep the business open until the end of the year. That way she could lessen the closing debt and perhaps, at least pay off the women and women's businesses to whom the Rue owed money. All the remaining collective members decided to leave and by October of 1983 the business became a partnership.

The Return to a Three-Owner Partnership

Katherine, a close friend of Alex, began thinking of involvement in the bookstore about the time the collective fell apart. She spent volunteer time at the business during the fall and by January of 1984 she became an official partner, although she had been participating in business decisions and meetings almost since the inception of the partnership in the fall.

Alex obtained funding from an undisclosed source in the late fall and was able to take care of almost $7,000 in business debts. At a meeting in November, attended by Alex, Laurie and Katherine in Alex's home, she went through the books and announced the bills that had been liquidated and those that had been significantly reduced and the balance owing. Women had been paid first. The spirit of optimism was apparent. Enthusiasm because of the coming holiday season and the release of financial pressure allowed the partners to speculate on plans for the future. Laurie and Katherine wanted to expand the kitchen facilities. Alex ordered new merchandise and Katherine added a line of incense and decals to the dwindling stock. The paid employee, Ann, prepared slow-moving merchandise for a sale and busied herself making a Christmas display. It was getting chilly and Laurie, who was a cook by profession, came in most mornings to prepare daily soup and specials.

The business had been out of the collective stage for only a few months, but already some significant changes were evident. First, business increased significantly. Katherine left her job and now worked full-time at the bookstore. This enabled her to upgrade the variety of food available. Feedback indicated that patrons were happier because they could always count on Katherine being there and she was a warm and funny person. Some patrons came in just to see her because they could count on a good time. Regulars increased their visits and food sold well.

Second, during this stage there was an increased affiliation with other groups, which Alex characterized as political. A planned, combined social evening with the Lesbian and Gay Student Union (LGSU) of the University of Utah, held in the Rue on the usually separatist women-only Friday evenings, is an example of that increased affiliation. Although, according to Alex, the Rue was still "a woman-only space 99.9% of the time."

Also, the previously clear-cut line between Women Aware and Twenty Rue Jacob was blurred slightly by an increase in involvement of common members. At one point Women Aware made a loan to the Rue during a difficult time and since that time the two organizations had increased activities together, such as a joint fund raiser and party which included an auction of donated art work.

Third, there was an increase in feelings of community. Partially this can be attributed to the fact that patrons could count on who would be working there. Organizational members often explained that one reason people came into the bookstore was to interact with other women. It was generally thought that if one could count on who would be there, more people were likely to come in. Another factor was the establishment of a food co-op at the Rue, which brought members in regularly to place orders and check on the latest co-op news. Alex also felt that during this time people were going through a "yearly bar burn-out" and seeking alternative social avenues.

Another significant change was the interest in
obtaining more business skills. The collective members
often spoke of increasing their business abilities,
even applying for government programs available through
the Small Business Administration. The three current
owners took steps in this direction. One partner took
business classes and another enrolled in a marketing
seminar.

The changes evident since the passing of the
collective structure were perceived as positive by both
owners and patrons. For the first time since I began
studying the business, talk focused on activity and
plans for the future rather than plans for 'going
under' or closing.

Ironically, four months after the change to a
three-partner system, on April 25, 1984, the owners of
Twenty Rue Jacob sold their equipment and stock and
closed their doors.

Twenty Rue Jacob

Twenty Rue Jacob was located about four or five
blocks from the downtown area of Salt Lake City, Utah.
The bookstore/coffeehouse was open Tuesday through
Friday from 11:a.m. to 6 p.m. It was closed on
Saturday for several months because the collective
members were "burned out," but it did reopen for
Saturday business. Most of the owners held employment
elsewhere during their period of involvement, although
one owner worked full-time at the bookstore.

The coffeehouse was open every Friday evening
during the academic year on a 'woman only' basis for
special activities. These might included poetry
readings, musical performances, political meetings,
discussion groups, art show openings or parties.
Classes in assertiveness training, poetry writing

workshops, classes in stained glass art were sometimes held in the evenings once the establishment was closed for the day. On occasion patrons were allowed to hold private parties in the coffeehouse, although usually everyone was invited to attend even private functions.

The coffeehouse/bookstore was housed in a small leased building that occupies a corner lot with parking for a few cars in back. The front door opened into the bookstore. Two small front windows housed book or pottery displays which were changed periodically but paid little attention. A string of bells attached to the front door announced the arrival of customers.

Directly across the room from the door was a large bulletin board which serves as a communication center. The right third of the board was filled with business cards of women patrons, therapists, chiropractors, artists, lawyers, printers, and notes penned by women offering music lessons, French lessons and trade skills, such as carpentry, plumbing work and so forth.

The rest of the board was filled with announce- ments of community functions, both lesbian and feminist in orientation (Dignity, Women's Resource Center, the Phoenix Transition Center, The National Organization for Women); petitions or lists for special orders; advertisements for roommates or jobs or personal notes for individual women; and clippings that might be of interest to community members.

A suggestion box and a box marked "Women Aware" set on a shelf below the board along with a variety of hand-out literature on organization memberships, the rape crisis center and copies of the Women Aware newsletter.

The records sold in the bookstore were feminist or lesbian in orientation. Artists, such as Meg Chris- tian, Margie Adam, Holly Near or Chris Williamson, who

record on labels of companies controlled and staffed
either totally or primarily by women, were displayed in
a rack to the right just inside the door.

Unfinished wooden bookshelves took up most of the
remaining space. The stock carried in the store
included popular lesbian literature, woman and child-
oriented health care texts, feminist political texts,
books of poetry (many of them self-published by local
women poets), and an assortment of popular fiction, art
books and general information books donated by a
community member who once owned a bookstore and closed
it down. Occasionally, a sex education instructor at
the university ordered her texts through the Rue and
usually a few of these were left setting on the shelf.
At one time the bookstore ordered some books oriented
to gay males and these were arranged on one shelf. A
Gaia's Guide (not for sale, but available for the use
of patrons), which lists lesbian and feminist es-
tablishments across the United States and Europe, sat
on one shelf by the counter.

One bookshelf was used to display an assortment of
t-shirts, some bearing the logo of the establishment.
Others displayed a variety of feminist slogans or
proclaimed political events or concerts. A dish full
of buttons with slogans on them sat on one shelf.
Someone once placed several buttons with the slogan
"Nuke a Gay Whale for Christ" in the dish and they were
removed and disposed of.

Both in the bookstore and the coffeehouse, the
works of women artists were displayed on the shelves
and walls. Included were pottery, jewelry, weavings,
paintings, woodworking, greeting cards and tie-dyed
shirts. Most displayed some lesbian or feminist motif
or theme. A framed poster of interwoven threads
bearing the words "sister threads--20 Rue Jacob" hung

on the wall in the coffeehouse. A limited edition silkscreen done by a bookstore patron and donated to the Rue sold out all of the 16 copies at $10 apiece.

A doorway to the right at the rear of the store led to the coffeehouse, and an open area in the wall allowed whoever was minding the kitchen to keep an eye on the bookstore as well. Two booths, two tables and a counter with six stools provided seating in the coffeehouse. For classes or Friday evening sessions, sixteen chairs purchased from a school district were brought into the room from their storage area in a roomy bathroom in the back.

Bright tablecloths and vases of silk and sometimes real flowers decorated the tables. Women's artwork hung on the walls around the room. Over the counter was a stained glass piece with the bookstore's logo etched in the glass. A blackboard menu hung at one end of the counter advertising such items as turkey, ham, vegie, and roast beef sandwiches, bagels, a soup of the day, nachos and vegi tostadas. For several months a variety of sandwiches bearing the names of noted feminists were printed on a lavender menu until collective members began to feel "burned out" with the chore of stocking and serving so much food and discontinued the menu and the sandwiches. When the sandwiches were reinstituted a few months later, the menu was not. An assortment of teas, mostly herbal, coffee and soda pop as well as a variety of juices were stocked on a shelf and in a cooler behind the counter.

Many women stopped in over the lunch hour for a bowl of soup or chili or a sandwich and to visit with friends. For awhile there were complaints that the menu items were "too vegetarian," but once the menu included meat in the sandwiches, complaints about the food offerings stopped. The most popular item was the

48

turkey sandwich on wheat bread.

Hanging above the window into the bookstore were about twenty mugs, identical except for the names printed on them. For $10 a woman could order a 'Rue' mug with her name on it from a local potter. The mug was left there on its hook for the woman to use when she came in. *Regulars*

Hanging on pegs behind the counter were identical aprons with the names of collective members silk-screened across the bib. They were ordered in a frenzy of enthusiasm and were seldom used. Several collective members took them with them when they left; however, some left them hanging there.

Located in a small hallway at the rear of the coffeehouse were two bathrooms. The women's room was the larger of the two and is kept stocked with toilet paper and paper towels and a stack of reading materials. A signed poster of a basketball star, Annie Meyer, hangs on the wall. Several posters of women musicians and notices of Rue activities hung on the walls.

The second bathroom, in contrast, was small and cluttered. It was difficult to get to because a vacuum cleaner, pieces of wood, and often a patron's bicycle blocks the end of the hallway. It served as a storage room for garage sale items, extra stock of paper towels, etc. It was used primarily as a second bathroom when the other was occupied since there are few male patrons. The sign on the door read "Others" until it was taken down because more men were coming in.

Clientele

Most of the regular clientele were lesbians. Two or three neighborhood children came in to purchase soda

Who

pop and an older man came in most mornings to have a
cup of coffee and read his paper. Often he would pick
up some of the papers setting around to read, such Off
Our Backs or Plexus, both feminist-oriented publications. The regular customers and collective members
considered him harmless. They used to feel at ease
with him and did not feel it necessary to monitor their
conversations when he was around until one morning he
came in with some pornographic photos of women to
share. The attitude toward him changed markedly for a
time. For some women his presence was tolerated, but
cautiously so. He often made remarks such as "Where's
your red shorts today?" or "Oh, you smell great - come
closer" that are heard as inappropriate by organizational members. He was usually trying to get someone
to take a trip to San Diego with him. People sometimes
made faces at one another when he came in, but for the
most part he was regarded as a 'lonely old man.'

The patrons ranged in age from around 16 or
17-year-old high school students to a 63-year-old
school teacher who had just retired and for the first
time felt free to 'come out.' The largest number of
women were in their twenties and thirties, some were
college students, others were blue collar workers and
there was a large number of professional women and
graduate students. Very few days went by that women no
one had ever seen before did not come in. In addition,
women from Idaho, Ogden or southern Utah dropped in
when they were in town. During the summer it was not
uncommon to have visitors from as far away as New York
or California. Most of these women had heard of the
business from friends, had read about the place in Ms.,
or had gotten the name and address from a gay guide or
by inquiring at the bars. Although some days went by
with very little business, others were very busy with

as many as thirty or forty women stopping in. For awhile a number of gay males were stopping by for lunch.

The establishment served a need in the community for those women who were too young to get into the local bars, for those women who were just 'coming out' and were hesitant to go into a bar, and for many professional women who preferred not to patronize the bars. It also served as a connecting point for women with children who felt they should do most of their socializing during the day rather than spend too much time away from their children. Several women brought their children in with them. The emphasis in the bookstore, then, was on the notion of community, and it is this notion that forms the basis of the ideological components I will examine in this study.

Serving such a variety of clientele made it difficult to design activities or carry an inventory which appeals to a wide cross-section of the potential population. Inevitably, much energy went into defining and redefining the current customers and identifying ways to appeal to potential customers, who were alternately described as straight feminists, gay males, or "anybody who wants to buy a book or have a sandwich."

Summary

Inasmuch as organizational members were committed to serving organizational goals that were feminist in orientation Twenty Rue Jacob can be regarded as an ideological enactment of feminism. There were clearly episodes which are best understood as feminist. One could ask, however, does the ideology justify the activity or does the activity provide an opportunity for the ideology? I am claiming the former, but realize

the possibility of the later. Because not just in the
conversations or organizational members, but in the
concept, formation, and development of the business and
in the physical setting and clientele, the organization
can be regarded as a production of feminist ideology.

In discussing the concepts of feminist business
and collectivism, and in providing a history of the
business, I have provided the necessary context for
this study. In the following chapters, I will examine
organizational discourse in terms of three ideologically relevant terms. In Chapters three, four, and five,
I look at conversations and rituals that enact different aspects of the notion of sisterhood, politicalism and separatism. In Chapter six, I examine the
implications of this study for the study of ideology in
organizations in general and feminist organizations in
specific.

[1]While this study deals primarily with radical feminists, most of the ideological base on which the analysis is based can be broadly defined as feminist. The concept of feminist business is a feminist, as opposed to a radical feminist, concept.

[2]Katherine Woodul, "What's This About Feminist Businesses?" in Feminist Frameworks (New York: Wm. Morrow, 1976).

[3]Katherine Woodul, p. 197.

[4]Katherine Woodul, p. 198.

[5]Katherine Woodul, p. 197.

[6]Katherine Woodul, p. 198.

[7]Axizah Al-Hibri, "Capitalism is an Advanced Stage of Patriarchy: But Marxism is Not Feminism," Women and Revolution, ed. by Lydia Sargant. Boston: South End Pree, 1981.

[8]Katherine Woodul, p. 198.

[9]An example of a feminist product which would be considered unacceptable might be any product which purported to support feminist ideals, such as posters, buttons, T-shirts, feminist toys, but which is produced and marketed by men. The same products, produced by women, would be considered politically correct.

[10]Katherine Woodul, p. 198.

[11]Jo Freeman and Carol Macmillan, "Building Feminist Organizations," in Building Feminist Theory: Essays from Quest (New York: Macmillan, 1980), p. 263.

[12]Katherine Woodul, p. 198.

[13]Jo Freeman, p. 263.

[14]Twenty Rue Jacob, the business under study, operated as a collective from May of 1982 to August of 1983. During that time, the collective consisted of between 5 and 12 members.

[15]Karen Brandow, Jim McDonnell, and Vocations for

Social Change, No Bosses Here (Boston: Alyson Publications, 1981), p. 9.

[16]Karen Brandow, p. 75.

[17]Karen Brandow, p. 75.

[18]Karen Brandow, p. 91.

[19]Karen Brandow, p. 79.

[20]Collective Meeting (5/11/83). House on Columbus Street.* (*The meetings from which quotations are used were held at the homes of individual collective members or in the bookstore.)

[21]A 1983 article in Ms. magazine quotes Carol Senjay of the Feminist Bookstore News as saying that eighty or so stores exist; however, in the September 1983 issue of her publication she states that over one hundred ten such stores receive her publication.

[22]Ms., September 1983.

[23]Ms.

[24]Observation Notes--Conversation in the Rue (3/10/83).

[25]"ICI Decision: Store Awarded to Locked-Out Four," Plexus, May 1983, p. 1.

[26]The 'coming out' process is described by anthropologist Deborah Goleman Wolf in The Lesbian Community as implying the gradual realization "that one's feelings about women are much deeper and more emotional and erotic than feelings about men; becoming aware that this is a manifestation of being a lesbian; coming to terms with the social role and its implication; and finally, publicly committing some act that irrevocable identifies one, to oneself and informed others, as a lesbian." p. 33.

[27]Alex is a pseudonym for the woman who is the original owner of Twenty Rue Jacob. This examination of the creation stage of the business includes numerous quotes from a tape detailing the early history of the organization. She recorded the tape May 19, 1983 beginning at 5:13 a.m.

[28]History Tape (5/19/83).

[29]History Tape (5/19/83).

[30]The Michigan Women's Music Festival is held annually
on private land in Central Michigan. It is a primarily
lesbian event and craftswomen sell their products,
workshops are held and women musicians perform on a
central state. Attendance usually exceeds 10,000.

[31]History Tape (5/19/83).

[32]History Tape (5/19/83).

[33]An explanation of the name of the business can be
found in Chapter 3.

[34]History Tape (5/19/83).

[35]History Tape (5/19/83).

[36]History Tape (5/19/83).

[37]Observation Notes - Conversation in the Rue
(3/21/83).

[38]Observation Notes - Conversation in the Rue
(10/17/83).

[39]Conversation with Alex at Fifth Avenue House
(4/14/83).

[40]Observation Notes - Conversation in the Rue
(10/12/82).

[41]Women Aware is a lesbian group that meets at the Rue
but is unconnected to the business formally. They
publish a monthly newsletter that has a mailing list of
approximately seven hundred women, but no more than ten
or twelve attend the meetings.

[42]Partnership Meeting - Fifth Avenue House (10/18/83).

CHAPTER III

SISTERHOOD

In Chapter two I discussed the concept of
community as the ideological base of the organization
under study. In this chapter I will examine the
concept of community as it emerges in the enactment of
sisterhood manifested primarily in relationships among
organizational members.

Actually, there are two aspects of the ideological
component of sisterhood that are relevant to this
discussion, the theory and the practice. Unlike
separatism, however, sisterhood is not perceived as
being inconsistent with theory in practice even though
the two aspects look somewhat different. The theory is
that all women are sisters by virtue of their common
dilemma. This is articulated by Lisa Leghorn and
Katherine Parker.

> Sisterhood, or a shared culture, means that
> each woman encountering sexual, racial or
> class exploitation in her work-life shares
> the same relationship to the male economy as
> her female peers, both at her paid work place
> and in her home. It means that each woman
> could benefit most by discussing her problems

> and experiences with women in similar
> situations. . . With these women she shares
> a common experience, culture and perspective,
> forming one of the variants of women's
> cultures.[1]

From this perspective, sisterhood is not only a reason
for or an end result of separatism, but a means of
formulating a collective identity. The feminist
concept of sisterhood emerged as a result of the
recognition of the estrangement women felt from each
other and from their history. One means of keeping a
group oppressed, feminists reason, is to rob them of
their collective identity. To claim power and thus
shake off oppression, women had to reconstruct that
collective identity. The first step was seen as
recognizing their common fate and letting go of the
issues that separate women from one another. This
previously unarticulated notion emerged in the modern
women's movement in the slogan "Sisterhood is
Powerful,"[2] adopted by New York's first women's group,
Radical Women in 1967 and used as a rallying cry during
the late 60s and early 70s.

The second aspect of sisterhood is located in
practice. It functions at the individual rather than
the collective level and is manifested on this level in
relationship. It is this aspect of sisterhood, how it
is enacted in interaction, that is the focus of this
chapter.

This analysis is clustered around four emerging
characteristics of the enactment of sisterhood at
Twenty Rue Jacob. Each of these characteristics is
stated in terms of a claim about what is going on.
First, there is little sense of a need to reconstruct a

collective identity in this organization. Rather than
being thought of as being constructed or in the process
of becoming, collective identity is assumed to exist a
priori. The recognition of the need to construct a
history (or herstory) is evident, but the collective
identity has existed all along. Second, enacting
sisterhood is often seen as being inconsistent with
"being a business" in much the same way that a tension
exists between separatism and business. Third, the
metaphor of family provides rich insight into
relationships in the organization. Its application is
unique in this organization because the idea of family
extends to a whole community rather than being limited
to relationships between organizational members.
Fourth, during points of ideological strain, when the
ideology does not seem to be working, organizational
members develop strategies for explaining what is going
on rather than entertaining new competing ideologies.

Collective Identity: An A Priori Assumption

The first claim I wish to make about the enactment
of sisterhood at Twenty Rue Jacob deals with the
concept of collective identity and the nature of
sisterhood in feminist and lesbian feminist theory.
For lesbian feminists in this organization[3] collective
identity is an a priori assumption. This is different
from a feminist conception of collective identity.
First, for lesbian feminists it is a category imposed
on them by the outside world. People might say, "Look,
there go two lesbians," but they would be unlikely to
say "Look, there go two women." This categorization is
taken for granted by organizational members. One
incident occurred when children threw rocks and yelled
'queer' at one customer. In another incident

organizational members were called 'faggots' by
neighborhood children. Their primary complaint was
that the categorization was wrong.

Second, for lesbian feminists collective identity,
and therefore sisterhood, is something that exists by
virtue of their world view. There are certain values,
ideas and beliefs that lesbian feminists share that
makes them sisters. The world view and the lesbianism
are assumed to be integral aspects of the same thing.
A deviation from some aspect of the world view might
cause one to question another's lesbianism. Sisterhood
is an inseparable aspect of the lesbianism. For
feminists, on the other hand, sisterhood is the
recognition of a relationship that exists by virtue of
a common condition. It is based on the "shared,
primary oppression of being female in a patriarchal
world."[4] The lesbian feminist views herself as doubly
oppressed - both as a woman and as a lesbian.
Sisterhood, in a lesbian feminist sense, begins with
this feminist conception - incorporating the ideas of
sharing, group consciousness, bonding with other women
and support - and then incorporates a romantic and
sexual dimension. "All women are my sisters, and some
are my lovers."

The nature of sisterhood is also different for
lesbians because lesbians do not feel estranged from
each other in the same way as other feminists. From a
feminist perspective the concept of collective
sisterhood is a vital aspect of historical identity.
Women have been pitted against each other and have
engaged in competition for the primary means of
economic, emotional and social survival for women-men.
The feminist recognition of this alienation from one
another provided a goal of group consciousness for

early movement radical feminists.

> Women are the only oppressed people whose
> biological, emotional and social life is
> totally bound to that of the oppressors. We
> must provide a place for women to be friends,
> exchange personal griefs, and give their
> sisters moral support. In short - develop
> group consciousness.[5]

Lesbians certainly consider themselves to be socially
isolated from one another, but they do not consider
themselves to have been alienated from one another.
The group consciousness was there in a psychic
connection - what was missing was a social connection.
For feminists, bonding is an active effort akin to
relationship-building. For lesbians, some relationship
exists prior to connection. It is this connection that
the Rue came into existence to provide. It was
perceived as a vehicle for actualizing relationships
that already existed.

> To look in the mirror and say, "I am a
> lesbian." There is nothing worse than for
> one person who has said that to herself, for
> a lesbian who has recognized her lesbianism
> to be alone; therefore we created Twenty Rue
> Jacob.[6]

Since the business provides a connection, failure to
patronize it is regarded as a matter of consciousness or
awareness. The community is 'out there.' The Rue exists to
bring it together, to make connections that already exist
explicit. For many patrons, the Rue serves as an access

point to what is perceived as a pre-existing entity. All
lesbians are regarded as potential Rue patrons by virtue of
their community membership and organizational members regard
support of the business as a community obligation. This
same obligation is not extended to feminists, even though
the bookstore is defined by members and advertised as a
feminist bookstore.

That the community is 'out there' ready to be connected
is further evidenced in the designation of an appropriate
symbol for as yet unmet lesbians. One Rue client coined the
term PLUs (people like us) as an identifier of individuals
perceived by community members to be lesbians. Another Rue
client recounted the story of an encounter she and her lover
had with two PLUs in the lounge of a local hotel.

> We were at the Hilton having drinks before
> dinner and uh, there were these two women
> sitting at the next table and they kept
> eyeing us and we kept eyeing them and I just
> know that they were (laugh) ya know? There
> were two guys sittin on the other side of us
> and I'm sure they were baffled by the way we
> were all checking each other out - anyway, we
> went over and invited them to join us for
> dinner. They were real nice, but they'd just
> ordered some nachos and stuff and were about
> to eat there. Anyway, we asked.[7]

In this interaction and in the listeners reaction to it
there is an assumption operating of some pre-existing
relationship prior to any social connection. Dorothy
Painter, in talking about an 'awareness' or recognition
factor that seems to occur between lesbians, attributes

it to a recognition of the familiar and the unfamiliar in others.[8]

This perception of women as PLUs or not PLUs affects the way they are dealt with as customers. I rarely saw anyone be rude to customers, but there was usually more of an effort to include PLUs in any casual conversation that might be going on or to ask them if they were new in town and give them a newsletter. Partly, this has to do with the idea that lesbians come into the Rue for one thing and nonlesbians for another. The assumption is that lesbians are there for a sense of community or connection, but that nonlesbians are there to buy books of food.

An important aspect of the construction of collective identity among feminists is the recon-struction of a women's history. This is also empha-sized by lesbian feminists. In a 1975 issue of _Win_ which focused on lesbian culture, one article dealt with the need for the development of a lesbian history as a means of regaining identity. "Without an histori-cal or cultural background people cannot authenticate their identities or provide role models which instill feelings of validation and self-worth."[9] At the Rue, however, the issue of history construction or recon-struction is not an important or active part of organizational life. One collective member served as an 'herstorian' for the business. Her duty was to keep a running record of what occurred as well as attempting to reconstruct the past. This task never seemed to be taken seriously. The last time I saw the herstorian files was when the collective member with that job left and returned them to the business. At that time they consisted of an empty scrapbook, some clippings and a lot of pictures in a box.

Alex, the founder of the business, was an exception to this. She occasionally would talk about a history of the Rue, making statements such as, "That's something I really want to do!" She did make an attempt to tape the history. The initial tape provided a detailed account of the business up through the first few months. The second tape centered around a few questions I asked in an attempt to reconstruct the history myself, but it did not provide a particularly clear or concise account.

In the Rue then, the notion that collective identity is an a priori assumption is manifested in 1) the idea that the Rue exists to provide a connection between women who are already sisters by virtue of the way they are socially categorized and their world view, 2) the notion that these women have an obligation as sisters to support the business and 3) the de-emphasis on the construction of an organizational history.

The Relationship Between 'Sisterhood' and 'Business'

The second claim I want to make deals with the tension that emerges in the enactment of sisterhood between being a business and serving the organization's ideological interests. The two concepts - business and sisterhood - are at odds with one another and are perceived as being contradictory.

Alex hints at this contradiction when she talks about seeking an increase in business skills, with one partner taking business classes and another enrolled in a marketing seminar. She notes the inconsistency when she seeks to reassure the listeners that "even though we're looking into the business side of things, the bottom line is community. I'm real aware," she says, "that without that sense of community, we wouldn't be there."

Conversation at business meetings is filled with a curious blend of 'business words,' such as productivity, hard-assed decisions, con game, responsibility, money, bills and real hard asshole; and ideological words, such as sisterhood, caring, sharing, talking to people, energy and collectivism.

The tension between sisterhood interests and business interests is evident in this business meeting interaction:

Alex: Um, one thing that I've heard a lot of is that the group suddenly is filled with negative energy, when people go in there they don't see smiles, they don't see positive attitudes and they don't feel good. They're not welcomed. Women, what that boils down to in the business world is the fact that we are not thinking of the customer and having the customer come first. If we are going to be a business we need to think about that. That is who pays the bills and we have to remember that and I know the old adage that the customer is always right. I don't believe they are always right, but we don't have to let them know that we don't think they're right. I know it's a con game, but selling is a con game. . . and I think if we want respect, we've gotta give it - and that's true. If you wanta be smiled at, goddamn it-smile at them. If you wanta have it, give it! And that's true, the attitude at the Rue is bad

from here, and I've been putting
myself in everything I say. It's not
good. It's too negative. It's not
productive and we need to look at
that. Why?

Alice: Yeah, well, I have something about
that. It's like, I've been nailed for
talkin to people, an' for sittin' down
and doin' my thing and ya know, I'm
not washin' dishes and stuff and
that's bullshit for me. I'm not in
that space. I need to do dishes. I
need to do this. I need to do that.
That's not where my energy is at.

Jane: That stuff can always be done after
hours when the customers are not going
to be there after hours.

Alex: See - you hit it right there. The
point is women, that if you want a
business to go, goddam it, if you're a
teacher, come on women, if you're a
teacher you don't do your damn lesson
plans during the school day, you do it
after school and before school and you
do it on the weekends, and you work
your asses off on the holidays. It's
the same with business. Why is it
that we think we cannot work past 7
p.m. or prior to 10:30 a.m. Why is
it? Why is it that we cannot feel
like it and be energized enough to put
in that extra five hours a week?

Alice: Well, this is what it is and I'm as
much to blame as is that individuals

> are doin, well, I want this, I need
> this, I cover my ass here and it's not
> the true spirit of collectivism.

Alex: That's right.[10]

There is only so much time and energy to go
around, some collective members argue, and both
interests are vying for priority. Alex, however,
provides an alternative explanation. The key is
commitment. The two concepts are not at odds with one
another, organizational members simply have to work
harder.

The ideological concept of sisterhood is dealt
with in this conversation in metaphorical terms. The
metaphor, that of teaching, is used to soften the
concept of business to include elements such as caring
and dedication. The implication is that aspects of the
ideology are essential, indeed, the key to the success
of the business. Applying a teaching metaphor to a
capitalistic enterprise 'humanizes' it, enables the
participants to conceptualize business success in more
palatable terms consistent with the ideology.

The process of 'getting at' what is going on in
the business, of exploring in the talk, the relationship between 'sisterhood' and 'business' leads to
first, a suggestion to abandon the ideology; then, an
attempt to synthesize the two elements; and finally, a
redefinition of 'sisterhood' in the experience of
organizational members.

There is a recognition here of the tension between
the concepts of business and sisterhood as well as the
dialectical tension between a utopian or idealized
conception of the ideology and the production or
enactment of it.

Alex: . . . and I think it's fucking about
        time. I really do. So I think that
        we need to make a decision - are we
        gonna stay open and is everybody going
        to pull their weight and I don't give
        a shit how we do it, or are we goin to
        close and share this responsibility
        and forget this touchy feely sister-
        hood shit that isn't working for us.

Jean: I'm glad you said that because I
        wanted to make a comment about what I
        think is part of the problem and that
        is that for many of us getting into
        this kind of business venture it was
        an alternative to working in a
        traditional system that was seen as
        oppressive and we wanted an alterna-
        tive feminist type business to be a
        part of and for some people I think
        that meant the sisterhood bond of
        touchy feely, let's be nice to each
        other, let's have a good environment
        to work in and I think and what's
        happened, even though those are nice
        idealistic things to have is that we
        have ended up pushing under the rug
        some of the hard assed decisions that
        are going to have to be made if this
        business is going to work, and some-
        times, dealing with anger or resent-
        ment or problems and with realistic
        kinds of things that are happening
        because people aren't wanting to be in
        a business environment that requires

> some kind of not so pleasant things to
> happen, we've gotta get out of that,
> it's nice to have sisterhood, but
> let's have some more organized
> activity. . . . .

Alex: Right.

Kay: That's right!

Alice: That's right and let's have some
business sense.

Kay: Sisterhood. (pause) I have a problem
with that. I don't think we've ever
had it.

Alex: We have a pseudo thing and I'm not
really sure of what it is - not really
sure.

Jean: Which is exactly part of the seduction
of touchy feely sisterhood bullshit -
is surface.[11]

A distinction is made here between 'touchy feely
sisterhood shit,' which they perceive as being enacted
("We have a pseudo thing"), and the idealized conception of sisterhood ("I don't think we've got it, I
don't think we've ever had it.") When the ideology
conflicts with the enactment, the explanation cannot
incorporate the inconsistency. Explanations have to be
formulated and the logical course if the ideology does
not work, is to reconceptualize what is going on as
inconsistent with the ideology. If what we are doing
does not work, then it is not the fault of the ideology, it is the fault of our enactment of that
ideology.

In these and other examples of interaction the
tension is evident and calls for a reassignment of

meaning to ideological notions and to organizational goals. When business is going okay, sisterhood -- providing a common connection -- emerges as the paramount organizational goal. It is talked about more, new projects to serve that purpose are undertaken, but when business is poor 'being a business' as a means of survival becomes the paramount goal.

Sisterhood as an Enactment of Family

The third claim I want to make about the enactment of sisterhood in this organization is that the application of a family metaphor is unique because it extends beyond the organization to the community and provides rich insights into relationships between organizational members and between organizational members and community members.

For lesbian feminists who can be regarded as cultural nationalists, the eventual objective of revolution is the establishment of a matriarchal society.[12] While this objective functions more as a dream in this organization, elements of matriarchy are evident in the family structure. Alex, the original founder of the business, can be regarded as both the material and ideological 'mother' of the business. In some ways her mother role is material because it incorporates taking care of or nurturing others. This is exemplified by her interaction with patrons in the coffeehouses.

1)   "Feed you? Oh, yes, it does my heart good to feed these women."[13]

2)   "Whatsa matter, huh? (puts her arm around someone's shoulder) Are you having a tough day?"[14]

Her role of mother is also evident in her expressions of concern for the group of younger women who frequent the business.

Alex: They've worked so hard to do that dance all by themselves.

Anne: Who?

Alex: The babies - they've rented all the equipment, selected all the music, made all the arrangements. I just hope it goes well. I hate to see them shot down.[15]

Since she functions as the organizational matriarch, it is not unusual for women, particularly the young ones, to develop 'crushes' on her. Women are often stopping by to see her and when the phone rings women often comment, "It's probably for Alex."

Even during the collective stage when there were twelve owners, the weight of decision-making often rested or depended on Alex. She was almost always consulted even during times when her involvement in the business was minimal. When she took a 'sabbatical' during the third year of business because she was burned out, she was called back because the collective was starting to fall apart and she was needed. Her absence was often noted, "I wish Alex was here." "She really should have come." "I wonder how Alex would react to that." "Perhaps we ought to ask Alex."

As the ideological mother of the business, Alex's relationship to Twenty Rue Jacob was different than the relationship of the other owners. Her intent was primarily ideological. "I never thought of this as a money-making business, we just wanted to stay one step ahead of the wolves."[16]

While other owners and collective members were
obviously interested in the ideological aspects of the
business, when they made the decision to leave, it
usually was articulated in terms of cost, either of
time, energy or money. "I feel like I invested in
something and didn't get anything back." "This was not
a wise investment." "You say you're in the Rue to make
money, and I'm into money, too, and the Rue doesn't pay
my rent."

Even Alex eventually acknowledges the difference
in her perspective on the business and everyone elses.

Alex: It took me a long time to figure out
        that I do come from a different place
        than you three, so far as the Rue goes
        and Jean has been trying to cram this
        into my head for months now.

Jean: I have?

Alex: Yeah.

Jean: What?

Alex: Because you've said things like that
        before, that well, 'It's your baby'
        and that kinda stuff and I've said,
        'Sure, sure, but it's true.'[17]

A family metaphor is also apparent in an incident when
two collective members discuss making the business a
beneficiary in their wills:

Gail: Well, this next thing is kinda morbid
        so I hope you understand. Uh, how
        would you folks like to start a
        homestead or a commune of some sort in
        Colorado some day? Well, there's a
        catch. And the catch is Sally and I
        are working on our wills this summer

and we've thought about it and thought
about it and if one of us dies then
the other person would naturally get
the property, but if both of us die at
the same time we think we should have
somebody designated for that instead
of having a lawyer do the estate and
something awful happen to it. We
hopefully shouldn't have a problem
because we don't have any siblings to
worry about - so we were wondering if
the Rue would take it if we wrote it
up in the will - actually you would
get both properties if we both died.

Alice: What if the Rue wasn't in business
anymore?

Gail: It would automatically disqualify it -
it would have to be. . .

Jane: I think that's a really generous
offer.

Gail: and we feel good about it - leaving it
to a woman's organization, especially
after all the work we've put into
it.[18]

Property can be regarded as progeny for lesbians
because many do not have children. The business here
serves as surrogate parents for what two women have
built together. What is going on is more than wanting
material wealth to be transferred for the sake of other
women. Gail talks about the property in terms of the
"work we've put into it," rather than in terms of
financial worth. The assumption is that the property
would be put to a family type use. She does not say,

"The land in Colorado could be sold and you'd make a
tidy bundle." Rather she talks about it in terms of
the potential use by the business in the same way that
she and her partner have thought about it - as something that has been built rather than a material
commodity. She says, "How would you like to start a
commune or homestead for women?"

Openness, trust, honesty and supportiveness are
all values or qualities one expects to find in a family
setting and each of these values is an important
aspects of sisterhood in this organizational setting.

Supportive communicative behaviors between
organizational members were frequent. "Here let me
make the sandwiches while you finish your Tab." "I'll
run and get the lights at Grand Central, I'm not busy."
"Here's a free sandwich - finishing your thesis calls
for a celebration." "I know this is a tough time, but
you have us. We're always here." These supportive
gestures are the norm. They provide a climate in which
conflict is rare and issues are often discussed on the
spot.

In addition, in the relationship between organizational members and patrons, supportive behavior is an
expectation. One patron told me, "People go to the Rue
for healing." It is regarded within the community as
one function, perhaps even the primary function, of the
business. In this way organizational members all serve
a strong and nurturing matriarchal role. This is often
mentioned as one reason for organizational member 'burn
out' at the Rue. "You spend all day pouring out energy
for other people and you just don't have any left for
yourself." The Rue is often talked about as "hard
work." It could not be thought of as hard work in
terms of the volume of work. Often hours went by with

only a few customers coming in. It was more the nature
of the work that made it a demanding job. An example
of one incident serves to illustrate this. I was
volunteering one afternoon: waiting on tables, making
sandwiches and answering the phone. About mid-after-
noon a well-dressed older woman came in the front door.
She appeared nervous and awkward. She entered the
coffeehouse area, sat down and ordered a cup of coffee.
I waited on her and then began to clear off the
adjacent table when she solemnly asked me if I could
take a minute to talk with her. I said, "sure" and sat
down in the booth across from her.

She told me her name was Judith, that she was in
her late fifties and that she had been involved with
women on and off throughout her life, but that she had
always kept her lifestyle a secret from friends and
family. All of her relationships had been fairly
isolated. She was alone now, had retired and was
drinking too much. Her therapist had suggested she
come down to the Rue, meet people and become involved
in a community. It had taken awhile to get up the
courage, but she was here.

I gave her a newsletter, encouraged her to attend
a number of activities and introduced her to the other
women in the place at the time. When I returned to the
Rue a couple of weeks later, she was working behind the
counter as a volunteer and she was beginning to show up
to Friday night activities. Occasionally, if she had a
strong support group, she would even venture out for a
night of dancing at the bar.

Judith is not the only woman encouraged by her
therapist to show up at the Rue. Such referrals are
common. Even the Gay Help Line and sometimes the
Women's Resource Center refer women to the Rue. At

times this can cause a problem because most of the Rue
staff is not trained to deal with very severe problems,
and sometimes disturbing phone calls are referred to
local therapists.

Sometimes women referred to the Rue became
regulars and supporters of the business with invest-
ments of time and/or money, but more often they show up
for a period of time, seek some emotional support and
then disappear.

There are also several expectations, characteristic of family expectations, evident in the
interaction. One is that women, particularly collective members will take care of interpersonal problems,
be responsible to themselves and others and honestly
share their feelings. This is effectively talked about
metaphorically at a collective meeting:

Jane: and people are sittin on shit, and
        it's like. .

Anne: that's right, that's right.

Kim: we're like a constipated group.

Sal: and we need to take a big shit
        (laughter and expressions of dis-
        gust)[19]

True sisterhood would enable people to openly and
honestly express their feelings, but collective members
are "sittin on shit," inhibiting productivity ("we're
constipated"). "Taking a big shit" or dealing with
backed-up issues would enable the group to produce a
truer sense of sisterhood. They would not have
obstacles and therefore would be more productive. This
link between sisterhood and productivity was made
earlier by Alex when she characterized the pseudo-
sisterhood as "too negative, not productive."

Another expectation is the sharing of responsibility among collective members. This emerges
clearly when a violation is perceived to have occurred.

Jane: Yeah, like today when I talked to you
on the phone and you said, "I don't
want to be here."

Alice: Yeah, I was pretty direct. I guess I
get really tired sometimes of, that
it's still just a couple people doing
everything. I guess it's always been.
Whether it's a collective of 12 or a
collective of 6, it's the same. .

Jane: It was like that. . . when it was a
collective of 12, too.

Alice: Yeah, there were just a few people who
did all the work. That was what I've
always seen and ya know, that's really
hard for me, because my dream was that
it wouldn't be like that. Especially
with a group of feminists, and it's
also interesting to me that one of the
people that like, when we were the old
collective, that one of the hardest
workers was the least feministoriented
out of the group.[20]

There is also an expectation of reciprocity in
terms of the community in general.

Alice: I think that one thing that's happened
to me as a result of the kitchen side
of the business. . . that's where I
really lost my idealism. . . because I
sorta had an idea that. . . you'd be
interacting with people that kinda had

similar ideas about society, hopefully
feminists, who are also possibly
lesbians. Right? And one thing I
found was that people didn't really, I
mean I had days that I was treated
like, you know, somebody in a Dennys,
or worse. . .

Jane: Like ya know, I'm here to be waited
on?

Alice: That's when I started to get really
disillusioned. . . I mean so many
times I wanted to say to those people,
'Look, I'm not gettin' paid to do
this. I'm here because I want us to
have something in this community.'
Okay, so maybe a sandwich costs a
little more here, but you know damn
good and well, that it's not just a
sandwich. It's not just the food
you're eating, it's paying for having
this whole building, being able to
have all of it.[21]

In many ways the Rue can be regarded as the
community enactment of a family core. People come home
when they need help, they are nurtured, often they take
but do not give, and then go on their way until they
need home again. The Rue appears to play much the same
role for the women of the Salt Lake lesbian community.

Strategies for Explaining A Violation of Trust

The final claim I want to make about the enactment
of sisterhood in the business is that when the ideology
does not seem to be working, when some deviation

occurs, organizational members develop explanations
rather than abandon the ideology.

In addition to providing a common direction
ideologies determine what is deviant and govern the
responses to deviation. Sisterhood in this organization
was expected to be the norm and when a violation
occurred, strategies were developed to provide
explanations and handle the internal threat to the
ideology.

One aspect of sisterhood involves the belief that
openness, honesty and trust exist between sisters. From
this perspective the male-dominated world breeds
distrust. The ideal of sisterhood implies a trust
between women: men usually violate trust, straight or
nonfeminist women can be expected to violate trust if
men are involved, but sisters trust sisters. A
violation of trust then is perceived as a threat
because it interjects male values into the community
and threatens its uniqueness.

Communication strategies are employed in defining
the situation, reframing its context and dealing with
it in terms of the ideology. Two incidents of theft
occurred in the organization just prior to the
beginning of the collective phase. The most probable
explanation was that a patron of the organization was
involved. The first incident involved money taken from
a paper-covered coffee can used as a receptacle for
tips and donations. It was usually kept on the counter
in the coffee-house, which was accessible only by
coming through the bookstore. An undetermined amount of
money had disappeared and Amy and Carol (two owners)
and Sue and Kim (patrons) discuss the theft:

Amy: I can't believe the donation money
        walked off.

Sue: It had to be someone who is in here a
        lot since it was behind the counter.

Carol: Should we restrict people more? I
        mean. . .

Amy: No! No, we can't do that.

Carol: Yeah (pause) It must have been
        someone who needed it. (pause) I just
        wish she had felt free to ask.

Sue: What about the kids across the street?

Carol: I don't think so - I don't recall
        seeing them behind the counter or
        anything - besides the table is high.

Kim: Hey, remember the day we had people
        helping with sandwiches?

Carol: Yea, maybe, maybe then. (pause) I
        don't think I want to know - they were
        all friends.

Kim: Me either. If it was a friend she
        must have had a desperate need. . . to
        do that to her friends - sisters. I
        think she'll pay for it.

Sue: I think you oughta watch people more -
        Keep them from behind the counter

Amy: No, this is a second home to a lot of
        women. I won't restrict anyone,
        everyone because of one person. We
        want women to feel comfortable coming
        back and pouring their own coffee for
        themselves. If we lost money, I guess
        we lost money, but I won't change
        because of one.[22]

The same theft is later discussed in an open
letter written by a Rue patron to the community and
published in the Women Aware newsletter.

> Finally, I am extremely disturbed at the
> womon/wimmin[23] who ripped off the tip money
> from the Rue. My guess is that you have
> utilized the resources that the Rue has
> provided (or you wouldn't have taken the
> liberty of going into the back room - and
> therefore been trusted to do so) and should
> be aware of how important it is for us to
> have a place like the Rue in our community.
> No matter how poverty stricken you are, I
> find it selfish. You are not stealing only
> from the owners of the Rue, but all of us -
> the wimmins community. For if the wimmin of
> the Rue can't pay their bills, we don't have
> the resources of the bookstore and cof-
> feehouse anymore.[24]

The scope of the violation is evident in the newsletter excerpt. The threat is perceived in terms of
the whole community. The possible loss of a resource
involves stealing from "all of us - the wimmins
community." Yet Alex, even though such violations
threaten the business, has no intention of changing
things to accommodate violations. Denying access to
the area behind the counter changes the nature of
things. Restriction is a violation of trust, which is
an essential aspect of sisterhood. At this point, the
ideology is more important than the business.
    The writer of the letter specifically defines the
incident as a violation of trust. The theft is not a

threat in and of itself - only in its meaning in a
larger context. The estimates of the cash amount taken
ranged from $10 to $15, but the damage the incident can
cause to the organization is great. Alex, in talking
about her decision to sell her partnership to three
individuals reveals the impact of the thefts on the
system. This decision was made after the second theft
which involved breaking and entering and the loss of
jewelry, meat and cookies.

> I guess it was the thefts that did it to me.
> I mean this wasn't meant to be a heavy profit
> business. Our objective was to keep just one
> step ahead of the wolves. I didn't perceive
> of the wolves as people so close to us. It
> was for the women that I quit a decent job
> and gave up my savings for. . . I'm tired of
> working myself silly and not having the
> support of the community, so if they want it
> - let them invest in it. If nine investors
> can't be found by the end of June - we'll
> sell.[25]

Explanation strategies emerge in the interaction.
Initially there is a reluctance to admit that someone
took it when Amy expresses disbelief that the money
"walked off." Attributing more worthy motives to the
thief than the basic motive of greed is one means of
explaining the incident and softening the violation.
This may have been a violation of trust, but "it must
have been a sister who needed it." Even the letter
writer makes the assumption that the motive was need.
"No matter how poverty stricken you are, I find it very
selfish." The violation is not in the loss of the

items as much as in the fact that the thief did not ask
for help if she needed it. Undoubtedly, if she was in
need of food, she would have been fed. Another explanation strategy involves the perception of women as
victims of a male-created value system. A sister gone
bad is one who adopts male attitudes such as disre-
spect, distrust and greed. Alex exhibits this perspective in talking about the second theft in which the
offender broke a window to gain entrance.

> The reason we think it was a woman is that
> there were still some symbols of basic re-
> spect. All the cookies and meat were gone
> and the speakers were taken down, but not
> taken. The broken window pieces had been
> neatly stacked beside the trash can. No guy
> would have done that and they tried to pry
> open the jewelry case with a pen. A guy
> would have smashed it on the floor, broken
> the glass or taken the whole thing.[26]

Alex is assuming in her perception of the event, that
there are still some elements of sisterhood - respect
is there even if trust is gone. Alan Meyer, in studying
ideology in hospitals, found that ideologies guide
organizations' responses to external threats.[27] This
incident indicates that the same may be true of
internal threats. There were three basic responses to
the thefts.

First, there was an effort to reaffirm sisterhood
by seeking support from the community and from organizational members. Despite the fact that the losses
were minimal, three benefit events were scheduled to
assist the organization financially. A rummage sale

was organized and people were asked to donate items and to publicize the event; a beer party (kegger) and a Sunday brunch to be held in the coffeehouse were planned all within a few weeks of the thefts. These events were unusual in that they were designed as benefits rather than 'for profit' events even though only the rummage sale differed from the usual events sponsored by the organization. They served the purpose of bolstering the spirits, providing an ideological boost, as much as financial support.

Secondly, there was a determination that the organization would not change the system to accommodate or acknowledge the offender. Alex, in stating "I won't restrict anyone, everyone, because of one person. We want women to feel comfortable coming back and getting a cup of coffee for themselves. If we lose money, we lose money," suggests that the ideals must remain intact. Altering behavior, interjecting suspicion into the atmosphere of trust damages the concept of sister-hood.

A final and essential tactic is isolating the suspected offender in the talk. This serves the purpose of distancing the offender from the organiza-tion and the ideology. This is essential in defining the event as a violation of the norm and in continuing with current organization practices without feeling a constant threat. Immediately after the event, talk focusing on the thief regarded the offender as "a sister who needed it. . ." or "a friend" but as talk increased the offender was separated from the group by means of distancing talk. Organizational members began to refer to the "thief," or "whoever it was." Alex finally drew a sharp distinction between organizational members or patrons and violators:

> We have to rent everything. We certainly
> don't own anything -   Now, maybe if it
> wasn't for the untrustworthy asshole dykes
> who try to rip us off. . .[28]

In conclusion then, the enactment of sisterhood in
the business, Twenty Rue Jacob, is characterized first
by the assumption that a bond of sisterhood already
exists among women with a similar worldview and the
organization exists to actualize that relationship.
Second, business and ideological interests vie with one
another for the attention of organizational members and
sometimes creates confusion as to the role of organizational members in regard to customers. Third, Twenty
Rue Jacob can be considered a unique enactment of
family in that the founder and central figure in the
business serves as a material and ideological mother
for organizational members who in turn serve a similar
function in respect to certain segments of the lesbian
community. Lastly, when a point of ideological strain
is reached, rather than entertaining a new ideology,
organizational members develop explanations and
strategies consistent with the current ideology.

CHAPTER 3
ENDNOTES

[1]Lisa Leghorn and Katherine Parker, <u>Woman's Worth:</u> <u>Sexual Economics and the World of Women</u> (Boston: Routledge & Kegan Paul, 1981).

[2]The slogan "Sisterhood is Powerful" was first used in 1967 by members of New York City's Radical Women in a demonstration during an antiwar protest to engage the attention of other women. The slogan was later adopted by Robin Morgan (1970) as the title of her anthology of writings from the women's movement.

[3]Although I am only making this claim in relationship to the women in this organization, I suspect that it is true of lesbians in general.

[4]Lisa Leghorn and Katherine Parker, p. 20.

[5]Robin Morgan, ed., <u>Sisterhood is Powerful</u> (New York: Random House, 1970), p. xxviii.

[6]This is excerpted from a tape recorded by Alex concerning the early history of the business.

[7]Observation Notes - Conversation in the Rue (6/18/83).

[8]Dorothy Painter, "Recognition Among Lesbians in Straight Settings" in <u>Gayspeak</u>, ed. by James Cheesbro, (New York: The Pilgrim Press, 1981), pp. 68-79.

[9]June Rook, "The Need for a Lesbian History," <u>WIN:</u> <u>Peace and Freedom Thru Nonviolent Action</u>, June 26, 1975, p. 18.

[10] Collective Meeting - House on Columbus Street (5/11/83).

[11]Collective Meeting - House on Columbus Street (5/11/83).

[12]Lucia Valeska, "The Future of Female Separatism," in <u>Building Feminist Theory: Essays From Quest</u> (New York: Longman, Inc., 1981) pp. 20-31.

[13]Observation Notes - Conversation in the Rue (11/12/82).

[14]Observation Notes - Conversation in the Rue (5/16/82).

[15]Conversation while running errands - Alex's car (5/12/82).

[16]Observation Notes - Conversation in the Rue (12/7/83).

[17]Collective Meeting - House on Columbus Street (8/21/83).

[18]Collective Meeting - House on Williams Street (4/4/83).

[19]Collective Meeting - House on Columbus Street (5/11/83).

[20]Interview with a collective member in the Rue (8/5/83).

[21]Interview with a collective member in the Rue (8/5/83).

[22]Observation Notes - Conversation in the Rue (4/20/82).

[23]Alternate spellings of the words woman and women are often used by radical feminists as a means of eliminating the 'man' and 'men' which are part of the traditional spelling.

[24]Women Aware Newsletter (summer, 1982 issue).

[25]Conversation with Alex in the Rue (5/5/82).

[26]Conversation with Alex in the Rue (5/5/82).

[27]Alan Mayer, "How Ideologies Supplant Formal Structures and Shape Responses to Environments," Journal of Management Studies, No. 19, 1982.

[28]Conversation while running errands, Alex's car (5/12/82).

CHAPTER IV

POLITICALISM

In Chapter Three, I discussed sisterhood in Twenty Rue Jacob as the component of the ideology in which the notion of community becomes ideologically defined and enacted and the place where organizational contradictions are least pronounced and most successfully managed. Chapter Four deals with the second aspect of the ideology to be examined - politicalism. In this component, the internal contradictions become more pronounced at the ideological level and less successfully managed.

The analysis in this chapter is organized around three basic claims about the nature of the political aspects of the ideology as it emerges in the organizational enactment. These claims are rooted in the assumptions that organizational members make about the way things are and emerge in practice as contradictory. Organizational members regard their existence as political, but the enactment of that political nature is problematic in a capitalistic enterprise.

The first claim I want to make is that organizational participants regard their existence, and the existence of Twenty Rue Jacob as inherently political. The fact of existence <u>cannot not</u> be a political

statement or accomplishment. Given this first claim,
the second claim is that a contradiction emerges
between the political nature of the organizational
participants and the 'place' of the business in the
community. The third claim is that the political
aspect of the ideology emerges most clearly in times of
stress and provides explanations for actions and
possible responses to crisis situations.

The Business as a Political Entity

To the outsider who wanders in, browses through the
books and sits down for a cup of coffee or herb tea and
cheesecake, there is little in the organizational
setting that would characterize Twenty Rue Jacob as
'political.' Mostly it seems like a quiet bookstore/-
coffeehouse where one can buy a book and settle down
for awhile to peruse it. Occasionally, posters for ERA
rallies or anti-nuke campaigns are hanging on the door
or walls along with posters for concerts or seminars.
Sometimes petitions concerning cable TV or birth
control issues are set out on the counter, but this is
really not any different than many other bookstores in
the area. Similar posters and petitions can also be
found in bookstores near the university and downtown.

The nature of the books and records available
characterize the place as different, but few would
regard the difference as political, and yet organizational participants regard their personal existence and
the existence of the bookstore as inherently political.
In fact, existence <u>cannot not</u> be regarded as a political accomplishment. This claim is rooted in the
assumptions organizational members make about the
political nature of their relationship and the relationship of the business to the society in which they
exist.

The assumption that the business, Twenty Rue Jacob, is a political statement is grounded in the lesbian identity of the organizational participants. Lesbianism is regarded by lesbian feminists as a response to patriarchal oppression. To facilitate an understanding of this political stance, I will provide a brief description of how lesbianism is conceptualized as political by radical feminist writers.

In the early '70s, when the current women's movement was developingstrength, lesbianism became, among radical feminists, a "way of combatting the overwhelming heterosexual ideology that perpetuates male supremacy."[1] The lesbian feminist, according to Alison Jagger, believes that "ones sexual choice attains tremendous political significance."[2] All relationships with men were seen as essentially political and sexual relationships with men amounted to "sucking up to the oppressor." The lesbian feminist contention is that "since the lesbian actively rejects that relationship and chooses women, she defies the established political system."[3]

This viewpoint was strengthened when radical feminists, both lesbians and nonlesbians, began conceptualizing lesbianism as a tactical response to male supremacy. Radical feminists asserted that until women could grant other women equal status with men, "until (they) see in each other the possibility of a primal commitment which includes sexual love, they will be denying themselves the love and value they readily accord men, thus affirming their second-class status."[4] This political stance was more than theory, it became practice, and many radical feminists joined the lesbian ranks to fight male supremacy. Today the political aspects of lesbianism are more often assigned retro-

spectively. Few consider the motivation of their
initial involvement as political; but most organizational members would very definitely assign political
meaning to their lesbianism. This stance, the conceptualization of their lifestyle as a political statement, while it is an assumption of most organizational
members, is not as prevalent among the patrons of the
organization, and to many, particularly the younger
women, it may be a new idea.

The recognition of this political relationship
between the lesbian and society was operating even in
the founding of the business. Alex makes this clear in
discussing the plans for the formation of the walk-in
business:

> We . . . decided there was nothing more that
> we could offer this community. . . than a
> place for women to meet. . . to see what the
> political aspects of being a lesbian are.
> Not the radical political aspects, I mean the
> fact of stating to yourself one morning, of
> looking in the mirror one morning and saying
> "I am a lesbian." That is so political. It
> is not a march on the capital or letters to a
> senator about laws or having it tatooed on
> your forehead and walking down the street, it
> is not one of those things, but it is one of
> the most incredible statements one can
> make. To look in the mirror and say "I am a
> lesbian."[5]

In drawing a distinction here between what she calls
the "radical" political aspects of being a lesbian and
the political 'fact' of being a lesbian, Alex is

characterizing the political stance as nonactivist.

The recognition of the political nature of lesbianism is part of the work of the bookstore - "To provide a place for women to see what the political aspects of being a lesbian are." It is here that a contradiction begins to emerge, because Alex initially characterizes the business as nonactivist by saying "not the radical political aspects" which she describes in activist terms - "a march on the capital or letters to a senator about laws or having it tatooed on your forehead and walking down the street." But, if individual lesbians are regarded as political, how do you avoid the conceptualization of collective, organized lesbians as being a political entity?

That she herself is unsure of the nature of the political aspects of the business is evident when Alex talks about the role of the Rue in the community:

> Up to now, here in this valley, we've functioned like social isolates. We have no power, no opportunity to make an impact, uh, even on feminist organizations, and a lot of us are really lonely.[6]

There is a general dissatisfaction with the way things are in the community. Alex talks about the dual role of the business as providing a political and social organizing force. It is the nature of this dual function that is at the heart of my second claim.

The Nature of the Business in the Community

In this business, in the community context in which it operates, the dual social and political function is problematic because the community is essentially

apolitical, and in some respects, antipolitical.
Lesbians, whether they consider themselves political or
not, nonetheless locate themselves outside mainstream
society, and some of them are therefore leary of
anything that draws attention to their existence. To
compensate for this element, the social aspects and the
political aspects of the business are balanced within
individual situations and the contradiction is either
managed by strategies which deny the inherent political
nature of the business or explicitly recognized:

> Jane: (nervously) Well, I think they think
> we're too political.
>
> Ann: (frustrated) What do they mean by
> that? Where do they get that idea?
> What have we done that's political
> since Political Lesbians met here?
> Name something? We're a bookstore and
> coffeehouse! Is that political?
>
> Carol: It's the political thing.
>
> Sue: We're not political.
>
> Carol: Oh, yeah?
>
> Me: Where does the political thing come
> from?
>
> Alex: (shrugs shoulders)[7]

This contradiction within the organization as to the
political nature of the Rue extends to the way it is
conceptualized within the community. Twenty Rue Jacob
is regarded by many as a political entity. Often this
is articulated in terms of elitism. I had the following conversation with one woman in a bar:

> Woman: Oh, I went in there once. They're a
> bunch of elitists.
>
> Me: Were they unfriendly?

```
Woman: No, but they think they know
        everything.  They're too political.
Me:     What made you feel that way?
Woman: I don't know, probably something
        somebody said.[8]
```

organizational members often express bewilderment that
they are perceived that way by the community and seek
explanations to explain that perception. In discussing
the problem, one owner, Carol asks another, Jane, why
she thinks that impression exists?

```
Jane:  Somewhere along the line they got that
        image, where, I have no idea.  They
        say, Oh, yeah, I've heard of that
        place.  That's what they say.  I've
        said - "Come in there when I'm
        in there - you'll see it's different."
        Now, I don't think there's a political
        thing so much anymore, but I got the
        feeling sometimes going in there -
        that you had to knowsomething to be in
        there.
Carol: Why was that happening?  What were the
        dynamics in there at the time you felt
        that way?  What gave you that impres-
        sion?
Jane:  I guess mostly Sally - because she
        would be talkin' about books and
        talking about different - because she
        is political, ya know, and she'd be
        talking about something and I'd
        overhear a conversation about somebody
        who I'd never heard of or some book
        that I'd never heard of.  Ya know, and
```

it was like - shit, I don't know
anything about this. Maybe I should
go look it all up. I wanted to go out
and party - and I felt like those were
the kinds of conversations that were
going on about a great new book that
they'd gotten that was this, that or
the other thing or somebody who'd made
a speech about something or other, and
I had no idea what was going on, and
I'd think 'whoa' maybe I should just
sit in the corner and talk to somebody
else who doesn't know. That's hard to
find in there when they're three
people.[9]

Jane's explanation cannot possibly account for the
perceptions of the community. Conversations on the
business are not often politically oriented and Sally,
the most politically oriented member, was only one of
twelve collective members. Alice, the collective
member who was the least feminist of the group,
probably had more one-on-one contact with people than
any of the others.

There are five locations in the organization where
the political enactment is evident: 1) the organizations logo, 2) the public statements of the business
owners, 3) the language of organizational members, and
4) the perceived support of political activities.

The organizational logo. A labyris, or double-
edged ax, reportedly the favored weapon of ancient
matriarchal societies, is the most prominent feature of
the organization's logo. It appears on business cards,
in advertisements for the business and on products,
particularly jewelry, sold in the store.

Inherent in the cultural nationalist stance
discussed in Chapter Three is the establishment of a
new society. Cultural nationalists speak of returning
women to the power they supposedly held under the
"grand matriarchies of prehistoric civilization."[10]
Alison Jaggar, in an assessment of political
philosophies of the women's movement, discusses lesbian
separatism in terms of this matriarchal orientation:

> Some lesbian separatists. . . argue
> explicitly for a matriarchal society which is
> an 'affirmation of the power of female
> consciousness of the Mother.' Such matriar-
> chists talk longingly about ancient matriar-
> chal societies where women were supposed to
> have been physically strong, adept at self-
> defense, and the originators of cultural
> advances.[11]

As the weapon of these ancient matriarchies, the
labyris emerges as a primary political symbol. To the
community at large, regardless of how aware of the
history of the symbol an individual might be, the use
of a weapon on the organization's logo makes a statement that the Rue and therefore the women of the Rue,
are in some respect political or as one woman who was
not a regular patron put it, "radical."

Within the organizational setting the labyris
serves two important functions: 1) it symbolizes
resentment and hostility and 2) it serves as a recognition symbol.

The idea of political activism is evident in
comments regarding possible uses of the labyris or
expressions of desire at owning one. It becomes a

means of symbolizing resentment and hostility toward
social inequality and male supremacy. While sitting
and having lunch one day with several women in the Rue,
one woman recounted an unpleasant encounter she had
that morning with a male co-worker.

> I just couldn't believe he was saying
> that. . . after all the work I'd put in on
> it. (shaking her head) I wish I'd had a
> labyris![12]

Another time there was a minor encounter with a man who
came in seeking some unusual information. After he
left, one organizational member declared, "I should've
asked him if he knew what a labyris was."[13]

The symbol also functions as a recognition symbol.
Many organizational members wear a labyris symbol in
jewelry form, usually on a chain around their necks.
That someone is wearing a labyris identifies them as
'lesbian.' An incident that occurred one afternoon
illustrates this principle. Two women, who no one had
seen before came in, looked around, purchased some
books and ordered lunch. Organizational members
interacted with them, discussing the books they had
purchased and the length of time the bookstore had been
there and after an hour they left. The following
conversation occurred after they were gone:

Ann: They were nice!

Jill: I feel sure they were. . . ya know.
(laughing and nodding her head)

Ann: Well, one was wearing a labyris around
her neck. . . a gold one.

Jill: Oh. well. . .[14]

That settled the matter. The wearing of the labyris
identified her as a lesbian.

A story is told by one collective member about a
woman author from the midwest who was to speak at a
women's conference at the University of Utah. She was
to pick the woman up at the airport and entertain her
in her home during the conference. Over the phone the
author described herself as a middle-aged, dark-haired
dumpy Jewish woman, but, she said, "Don't worry, you'll
recognize me." The collective member was somewhat
concerned as she and a friend watched the passengers
deplane. She described the scene:

> Then out came this woman wearing khaki pants,
> a baby blue chamois shirt and grinning
> broadly. Her chest was stuck out and around
> her neck was this huge silver labyris. It
> must've had a blade span of 4 inches. It was
> great![15]

The assumption operating here is that the symbol is
unique and foolproof. It is a sure sign of one's
lesbianism and it is discreet in that it is not readily
recognized by outsiders. It signals that the wearer
has a similar 'worldview.'

One organizational member, Ann, speaks with pride
of the beautiful picture of a labyris she has framed
and hanging in her office. Not long after she had hung
it, one puzzled male colleague made the comment, "Why
do you have a 4th century, double-edged, Mesopotamian
ax hanging on your wall?" Ann was astounded that
anyone would recognize the labyris and frequently
retells the story whenever the subject comes up.

Within the organization then, the labyris serves important functions for members, but to the community its presence in the logo signifies that the business and its members are politically radical. I asked one woman who was not a Rue patron, "What do you suppose this ax on the ad means?" "Well," she said, "it obviously means they're into revolution or women's rights or something. I mean, it's a weapon, isn't it?"[16]

Public statements. The public statements of the business owners are another location for the enactment of the political nature of the business. Very simply, the community regards Twenty Rue Jacob as political because the owners say it is political.

In April of 1983, a Statement of Philosophy printed in the Women Aware newsletter concludes with this assertion:

> We share with each other the belief that 'the
> personal is political.' For the collective
> this business is a political statement. We
> are working to provide you, our customers, an
> alternative to the often oppressive tradi-
> tions and standards of a patriarchal society.
> We hope that you will help us toward this
> end.

The political nature of the business was even a consideration when, in April of 1984, Alex decided to try to sell the business. The notice posted in the Rue announcing her decision and seeking a new owner stated:

Interested Parties Must:

1.   Be women.

2.   Have a vested political interest in the

SLC's community.

3.   Be willing to work hard for little return.
These public statements leave little doubt that the
owners consider the business a political 'entity' and
that even if it is to be continued by someone else, it
should remain that way. That the political nature is
inherent in the business is evident in the requirements
for potential new owners.

Language. A political stance is reflected in the
language used by organizational participants which
focuses on the relationship between themselves and
society. Organizational members refer to themselves as
'lesbians' or 'dykes' as distinguished from the term
'gay women.' Joseph J. Hayes notes, in his examination
of the language of lesbians and gay men, that:

> Presently, most activist lesbians have cast
> off the terms homosexual and gay as being
> male-marked. . . in favor of lesbian, which
> is quite clearly and solely female-marked.
> Moreover, some lesbians have decided to
> rehabilitate a formerly debased term, 'dyke',
> and turn it into a word that connotes
> strength, defiance and self-affirmation.[17]

To many segments of the community, this distinction,
particularly in regards to the term 'dyke', marks them
as political activist.

In a discussion of plans for the new image of the
business, three owners discuss the part that language
plays in the decision of some community groups to not
patronize the business:

Carol: I want everyone to be, to feel welcome
         in there. Right now I don't think

the black women feel welcome in there.
I know that. . .

Susan: How would you make them feel comfortable?

Carol: Yeah, that is true - because they're
not political and they have no reason
to be political. There's very few
that consider themselves lesbian.
They consider themselves 'gay.' Black
women don't consider themselves
lesbian - not the ones in Salt Lake.

Susan: What's the difference?

Carol: Because to them - lesbianism is this
big white thing. They really do
because I've talked to them about it
and they don't feel like - um, if they
say they are gay then they can
associate with men and most of the
black women I know go down to Fame and
dance with men on Friday night and
then go down to P and B and dance with
women on Saturday night, and they end
up going home with women or whatever,
but they have men in their lives, and
they don't want anything to do with
ERA or politics or anything like that
because their lives are in enough
jeopardy being a black woman, but
being a black gay woman puts them in
double jeopardy and so they don't
really want to be in there because
they don't want to be around political
stuff - they want to be around
comfortable, atmosphere stuff.

Susan: So who told them it was political?[18]

The term 'lesbian' then, to at least some segments
of the community suggests a separatist, and hence
political, orientation. Susan here does not see the
connection between the use of the term and the perception of the black woman of the Rue as political. What
Carol is saying here is that the black women in the
community are involved in a black struggle, so they
avoid the Rue because they feel that patronizing the
business is a political thing to do. If the Rue is
perceived as political by nonpolitical members of the
community, then patronizing the business may be
construed as an indication of a political stance or
orientation.

Another example of politicalism in language is the
alteration of the spelling of the term 'women' to
'wimmin' or 'womyn.' This is accomplished by organizational members in signs in the business, and notices
and columns published in the Women Aware newsletter.
This alteration in the spelling is viewed as a means of
"getting some of the power back" from men. As long as
the term 'men' or 'man' is embodied in the word
'women,' it implies, to radical feminists, that women
are 'of men' or 'belong to men.' This change in
spelling is not consistent and whether or not the
change is made and what form it takes varies with the
writer.

Political activities. The support of political
activities by organizational members is another
location for the emergence of a political orientation
in the business. The meanings assigned to that
support, however, differ among nonpatrons, patrons and
organizational members.

Within the community it serves, as well as among organizational members, the bookstore/coffeehouse is regarded as a political entity, more because of its ideology, its perspective on its place in the community and the political nature of lesbianism, than because of the actions or events it engages in. Although these events do tend to reinforce the political meanings people have already assigned to the business: the existence of posters for politically-oriented events, the enlisting of signatures for petitions (planned parenthood, cable TV), and even participation in community-centered events sponsored by nonprofit organizations, such as public radio and a feminist transition center all contribute to a perception of the business as politically active.

This community orientation often is perceived as exhibiting a political orientation. Examples include involvement in the Women's Conference at the University of Utah in 1982. Twenty Rue Jacob sponsored a booth, hosted an autograph party, advertised in the convention program and planned their activities (a dance and a breakfast) to coincide with the conference. This involvement was conceptualized as political because of the emphasis on women's rights.

Some organizational activities are more directly politcal. During 1982, the Rue served an active part in the campaign of one community member who was running for a state legislative office. One organizational member served as the campaign manager, others worked on posters, sold buttons or helped with the door-to-door campaign. An article in a <u>Women Aware</u> newsletter during 1981 gave a full account of planned activities of the local NOW chapter in support of the ERA. The article, written by an organizational member who was

president of the local NOW chapter, urged active
participation:

> If you are interested in performing, want
> more information, want to help us put up
> fliers and posters, or want to act as a
> marshal at the rally and/or march, the number
> is . . . Be there or be square.

Organizational members explain the ambiguity of
the situation, the contradiction that emerges as a
result of their nonpolitical 'political' involvement by
reconceptualizing the political nature of the business
as a vehicle for nonorganizational members' political
activities. Just as the Rue functions as a place for
women to develop themselves culturally, it serves as a
place for women to develop themselves politically. In
one business meeting, Alex said:

> We don't have to be radical. We just have to
> be a place or a vehicle for women who want to
> be self-motivated or radical orpolitical to
> do something, and that is what I see.[19]

The place of the Rue in the community - The
position of Twenty Rue Jacob in the broader lesbian-gay
community is ambiguous. Active feminists, in general,
regard the Rue as a place to gather, talk and have a
cup of coffee, while many nonpolitical members of the
community regard it as a very political environment and
therefore something to avoid or approach carefully.
This contradiction in perception is made explicit
in a conversation between Alex and a patron:

Diane: I have never looked at the Rue, even
      when I first started going in there,
      as, uh, an activist organization -
      never saw it as political.

Alex: You don't, but those black women do,
      those women at the bar do, those women
      at the Girl Scout Council do, the
      women at the Phoenix Institute do.

Diane: but I don't see that. . . but I guess,
      how do you get away from that when
      being lesbian is a political stance...

Alex: and that's the only stance, I think,
      that we can take and survive. If they
      want to take it from there, that's up
      tothem. If they want to organize
      groups and meet there, that's up to
      them, not us.

Diane: I mean, it's not like when the collec-
      tive was there, everybody turned up en
      masse to political rallies or any-
      thing.

Alex: Political stuff in this city is frigh-
      tening. The ones who have been the
      most radical are the ones who were on
      their way to someplace else. . .
      passin' through and they passed
      through and they went and they left
      and here we are - here I am and this
      is where I live, and here I am.[20]

What Alex is saying is that in the conservative
atmosphere of a city like Salt Lake many women prefer
to live "in the closet" and therefore anything that
draws attention to their private lifestyle is a threat.

Secrecy is a strong value among lesbians and particularly among Salt Lake City lesbians.[21] In this
kind of environment patronizing the Rue is regarded as
a form of 'coming out,' acknowledging one's lesbianism.

In effect, being ideologically based and providing
a vehicle for women who wish to be politically active,
effectively alienates many of the women that the Rue
wanted to attract. Many times during my involvement
with the business, I heard women say something like:
"If we were a bar and served beer we'd have every dyke
in the city in here."

Some segments of the community regard the Rue as
divisive because it is seen as separatist or elitist.
The Rue refuses to support some community events
because they oppose them ideologically. A member
describes one situation:

> The Royal Court, do you know what that is?
> Well, it's a gay organization, both men and
> women. They are boycotting our business
> because Women Aware won't support them.
> They're a sexist bunch. Put on drag shows
> and crown a drag queen and some dyke king.
> That sorta shit.

Providing an alternative to the traditional social
medium - the bars - is considered a daring and somewhat
risky venture. It upsets the status quo and poses a
threat to already existing businesses.

> Even Women Aware is hurt by the Rue. Women
> come to Women Aware a couple times, find out
> about the Rue and come in here all the time
> and stop going to Women Aware meetings and

activities. Same with the bars. We're all
competing for the same community. People
start going to one and stop going to
another.[23]

This places the Rue in a tenuous position. As a
feminist bookstore, it is regarded as separatist and in
a relatively non-political community, that makes it
radically political.

The Collective System: An Ideological Response to
Crisis

The third claim I want to make in regard to the
enactment of thepolitical nature of the Rue is that it
emerged clearly in a time of stress to provide explanations for action. The instance I want to examine is
the formation of the collective system as an
ideological response to a crisis situation.

In 1981, after Twenty Rue Jacob had been in
business for one year, a crisis was reached by the
three owners. Two of the women were working full-time
at other jobs and spending their evenings and weekends
in the business. Alex, who spent her days there and
often stayed to help in the evenings was carrying the
brunt of the new business. One owner, Sue, was
distressed because the time she spent in the Rue in the
evening was limiting the time she could spend at home
with her family. Then Carol, the third owner, met
someone and decided to move East with her when she was
transferred by her job. This left Alex and Sue to
manage the business alone. The two decided they could
expend no additional energy and they decided to close
and announced their intentions in the Women Aware
newsletter. The response was panic. Alex reports that

people pleaded with them to stay open. The need of the
community appeared strong: but the energy of the two
women was very low. The need was for more women to
become involved in running the business.

It was Alex who came up with the solution:

I've been doing some reading about collectives and that seems like the best solution.
So we've decided to go to a collective
system. We will be selling the three owner-
ships off and dividing them into three each
so that ultimately the business will be owned
by a collective of nine women. We'll be
giving it back to the community.[24]

Collective systems are discussed at length in
lesbian feminist writings. Feminist newspapers,
bookstores, social service agencies, all experiment
with the form because it is consistent with basic
feminist ideals. Many feminists have chosen to work in
all-women groups to "develop new feminist approaches to
problems,"[25] but the primary impetus, from a radical
feminist perspective, has been to provide a challenge
to the traditional hierarchal nature of organizations,
which is regarded as patriarchal and a means of
continuing the oppression of women.

The formation of the collective was explained
retrospectively as the solution to a number of
'problems,' the existence of which prior to the
explanation was problematic. The formation ceased
being explained in business terms - "no one had enough
money for the whole share," "no one could devote enough
time," "we needed the money, too," and began being
explained ideologically - "it was an alternative to a

traditional system," "we needed the input of a wider variety of women."

The ideological benefits of the alternative structure, such as providing an alternative work space, challenging hierarchical structure, providing a laboratory for feminist principles, were concepts applied to the action retrospectively. Organizational members made sense of it within the ideology using ideological reasons for the change. The reasons articulated prior to the change were business related rather than ideologically related -- the need for more people to work in the business setting and more money.

In addition, the ideological reasons given provided a selling point for attracting collective members. It would not have been easy to sell the Rue to people interested in becoming involved on a business level. It was not making much money and had already incurred a healthy debt. But since the primary reason for its existence was ideological, 'selling' involvement from an ideological standpoint seemed logical, and was far more apt to attract investors than the business status of the venture.

The formation of the collective structure at Twenty Rue Jacob, then, can be regarded as an ideological response to a business crisis. The reasons given by collective members for their involvement are primarily ideologically based. One collective member talks about the relevance of the structure for her and the woman with whom she shares her share:

> Getting into this kind of business venture,
> it was an alternative to working in a tradi-
> tional system that was seen as oppressive and
> we wanted an alternative feminist type
> business to be part of.[26]

In conclusion, I have made three claims about the way the political aspects of the organization's ideology emerge in the enactment of that ideology in the business. Organizational members regard the existence of the business as a political accomplishment, but this proves problematic in that the business serves or attempts to serve an essentially nonpolitical community. This contradiction imposes a mandate on the business - to change the 'political' conception of their existence, to enlighten the community, or to redirect their efforts. Efforts are directed, at different times and in different situations, to each of these. At times, organizational members deny the political nature explicitly in the interaction, at other times they explicitly state that purpose in hopes of enlightening the community and at other times, they attempt to redirect their efforts to a different clientele.

In politicalism, contradiction on the organization becomes more pronounced and explicit in the ideology. The notion of community itself becomes contradictory. How can the collective of women that make up the Rue be at odds with the community it exists to serve? The Rue is the political aspect of Salt Lake's lesbian community and exists to better the community's position and give it strength. Indeed, without the Rue, the notion of community itself becomes problematic because of the lack of any unifying factor. Yet, the business exists at cross purposes with a community which appears to want only a fragmented sense of community.

From the perspective of organizational members, the situation is analogous to the position of Alcoholics Anonymous in relationship to the alcoholic. The organization exists to better the plight of the

individual by providing community, dignity, and
self-respect. Rue members see themselves in a similar
way. The Rue is there to provide community, support,
collective strength and self-respect to a group which
essentially does not appear to want that. Organizational members, however, do not perceive that the need
is not there, only that the community does not see the
importance of having that need met. "They don't," says
Alex, "know how badly they need us."

CHAPTER 4
ENDNOTES

[1]Alison Jaggar, "Political Philosophies of Women's Liberation," in Feminism and Philosophy, ed. Veterling-Braggin, Frederick A. Elliston, and Jan English (Titowa, N. J.: Littlefield, Adams, 1977), p. 15.

[2]Alison Jaggar, p. 15.

[3]Lesbianism and the Women's Movement, ed. by Nancy Myron and Charlottee Bunch (Baltimore, Md: Diana Press), 1975, p. 30.

[4]New York Radicalesbians, "The Woman-Identified Woman," Lesbians Speak Out, ed. By the Women's Press Collective, 1971, p. 53.

[5]History Tape (5/19/83).

[6]History Tape (5/19/83).

[7]Partnership Meeting - Fifth Avenue House (10/15/83).

[8]Conversation with a woman in Puss n'Boots, a lesbian bar in Salt Lake City.

[9]Partnership Meeting - Fifth Avenue House (10/15/83).

[10]Alison Jaggar, p. 16.

[11]Alison Jaggar, p. 16.

[12]Conversation over lunch between three collective members (6/10/83).

[13]Conversation between two collective members in the Rue (8/12/83).

[14]Conversation between a volunteer and a collective member in the Rue (10/12/84).

[15]Conversation with two former collective members in their home (3/10/84).

[16]Conversation with a woman in the University of Utah Union concerning an ad for the Rue running in a local paper (3/12/83).

[17]Joseph J. Hayes, "Lesbians, Gay Men, and their 'Languages,'" in <u>Gayspeak</u>, ed. by James W. Chesebro (New York: The Pilgrim Press, 1981) pp. 28-42.

[18]Partnership Meeting - Fifth Avenue House (10/15/83).

[19]Partnership Meeting - Fifth Avenue House (10/15/83).

[20]Partnership Meeting - Fifth Avenue House (10/15/83).

[21]This was recently demonstrated (May-June, 1984) when a local prominent community member saw news reports about a lesbian athlete on the east coast who was suing a sports magazine for labeling her a lesbian. The local woman called the magazine's attorney volunteering to testify that she has seen the woman in a local lesbian bar several times the previous summer. The bar's membership list was subpoenaed but were reportedly burned before they could be confiscated. Her testimony in the case was perceived as the violation of a lesbian code of secrecy and trust. Business at the bar dropped to almost nothing for several weeks because members were fearful of the consequences of the publicity. Community members placed pressure on the bar to fire her from her job as a disc jockey, she lost her radio program, letters and petitions were sent to women's music personalities advising them that using her as a concert promoter would bring low attendance at their concerts and meetings were held in private homes to discuss "running her out of town."

[22]Conversation with Alex in the Rue (3/12/83).

[23]Conversation with Alex in the Rue (3/12/83).

[24]Conversation with Alex in the Rue (5/5/82).

[25]Karen Brandow, Jim McDonnell, and Vocations for Social Change. <u>No Bosses Here</u> (Boston, MA: Alyson Publications, 1981).

[26]Collective Meeting - House on Columbus Street (5/11/83).

CHAPTER V

SEPARATISM

In Chapter Three, I considered sisterhood in Twenty Rue Jacob as the ideological component in which community becomes defined ideologically and enacted by organizational participants. In Chapter Four, I discussed politicalism as the aspect of the ideology in which internal contradiction becomes more explicit at the theory or ideology level and less successfully managed. In this chapter, I talk about how contradiction is least successfully managed and most pronounced in the day-to-day life of the business in the concept of separatism. The analysis of separatism presented in this chapter begins with the assumption that in the same way that this business can be considered an enactment of feminism, it can also be considered an enactment of each of the ideological components. Sasha Gregory Lewis has referred to lesbian feminist collectives and organizations as "workshops of separatism."[1] It is in the practice, as evidenced in the day-to-day life of the organization, that theory is accomplished.

The analytical focus of this study is the communicative acts of organizational members and clients and the negotiation of meaning in those acts, both in terms of the individual and organizational understanding of separatism and in terms of the understanding of the theoretical concept. It is with the interface of theory and practice that this analysis is concerned and it is in the interaction of organizational members that the relationship between these two elements is constructed.

Adrienne Rich, in her assessment of separatist ideas in Sinister Wisdom, addresses the relationship:

> In trying to come to some clearer view of what separatism means, I have realized that for me, at least, theory and practice are constantly tugging at each other, often entangled with each other, but they are by no means the same. I find myself wondering if perhaps the real question at issue is not separatism itself but how and when and with what kind of conscious identify it is practiced. . .[2]

However, the issue of separatism is considered by many radical feminists to be dead. Lucia Valeska notes, "From the West Coast a friend writes that the very word elicits deadpan hostility or an active curse. Yet, she adds 'while so many are outwardly against separatism, they continue to live it.'"[3] Thus with the movement there is not simply confusion as to how separatism is enacted, but a question as to whether it should be enacted at all.

In this study, in an explication of the relationship between theory and practice in this business, I will address this issue and show how the dialectical tension between the idea and its enactment manifests itself communicatively and how orgnizational members deal with discrepancies between the two.

This analysis is clustered around three emerging characteristics of the enactment of separatism at Twenty Rue Jacob. Each characteristic is stated in terms of a claim about what is going on. First, the primary goal of this organization is to serve a function that can be termed 'separatist,' that of providing a place for women. Second, the enactment of separatism in this business can be characterized as cultural, as opposed to political. Third, the separatist goal of the organization is inconsistent with a business definition of the organization resulting in a separatist/capitalist dilemma.

What these claims mean in this organization is that organizational members, with widely differing separatist notions, are committed to a cultural separatist purpose which in this case is at variance with a business definition of the organization. As some of the women saw it, they were caught in a dilemma - they must either renegotiate their separatist purpose to remain a viable business entity or watch the business fail financially.

I will examine these claims and then show how organizational members go about avoiding renegotiating their goals by providing alternative explanations, compensating for contradictions and developing strategies for modifying change.

Separatism: The Nature of Theory

An examination of the nature of separatist theory is essential to an understanding of the confusion surrounding its enactment in the organization. I will examine the relationship of separatism to feminism, the

diversity of notions of separatism, and I will discuss
how these are applicable in this organizational study.

In "Some Reflections on Separatism and Power,"
Marilyn Frye characterizes feminism as kaleidoscopic -
"Something whose shapes, structures and patterns alter
with every turn of feminist creativity."[4] The one
element she sees as present in every change is
separatism and it assumes "different roles and
relations in every turn of the glass. . . depending on
how the pieces fall and who is the beholder."[5]

The theme of separatism, Frye says, is there in
every women's issue, "from divorce to exclusive lesbian
separatist communities, from shelters for battered
women to witch covens, from women's studies programs if
women's bars, from expansion of day care to abortion on
demand."[6]

That feminism is intrinsically separatist is a
claim made explicit in most discussions of separatism.
Feminism is, after all, a theory "that advocates a
culture of feminist values."[7] Most feminists,
theorists claim, practice some separation from males
and male-dominated institutions. In its mildest form
it is evident in the exclusion of men from all-women
activities and in its extreme form it is evident in the
lifestyle and politics of lesbian feminists.

With no clear fix on what constitutes separatism,
there can be no one right definition. Some see
separatists simply as those who consciously separate
themselves systematically as part of a conscious
strategy of liberation. Frye provides a very general
and often quoted explication of this definitional
aspect: Feminist separation is. . .separation of
various modes or sorts from men and from institutions,
relationships, roles and activities which are

male-defined, male-dominated and operating for the
benefit of males and the maintenance of male-privilege
- this separation being initiated or maintained, at
will by women.[8]

Of perhaps all the components of feminist ideology
and more specifically of lesbian feminist ideology,
separatism is the most elusive and least defined. No
spokeswoman has ever insisted on one definition. There
is no one correct feminist of lesbian feminist 'party
line' on the issue. There are only published personal
statements and explorations of the concept.

In this analysis, I will draw from those
statements in an attempt to determine some of those
things that 'separatism' means in lesbian feminist
ideology as a base from which to discuss the enactment
of separatism in this one particular feminist
environment.

Much as the theoretical understanding of
separatism, the understanding of the concept in the
organization under study is elusive. From my own
observations, I would say there is less shared
understanding among organizational members as to what
separatism should mean in the organization than there
is of the other ideological components under
examination. The primary reason for this being that
lesbian feminists, as well as radical feminists in
general, hold widely differing opinions on separatism.
Some would consider themselves radical separatists,
while others would not consider themselves separatist
at all.

Meanings are less explicit in the interaction and
revolve around the meaning of specific events more than
explicit discussions of the concept. I observed
organizational members discussing what 'sisterhood' was

and what 'political' was, but I never observed members
discussing explicitly the meaning of separatism.

Separatism was talked about in terms of who the
clientele should be, or who should attend Friday night
activities or should the 'others' sign be replaced with
a 'men's room' sign. Consensual meanings of separatism
were negotiated in these interactions. The focus was
on how separatism should be enacted in the
organization; how it should figure in decisions.
Usually, it took the form of a problem to be solved.
This confusion emerges clearly in an examination based
on the three claims I will examine in considering the
enactment of separatism in the organization.

Separatism and Organizational Goals

Separatism is regarded by lesbians as a purposeful
activity. It is not simply thought of as an act, but
is conceptualized as a 'process' having some end
result. Inasmuch as definitions of separatism are
grounded in discussions of purpose and articulated in
terms of reasons to separate, an understanding of how
separatism is enacted is best preceded by a
consideration of possible explanations of why. Three
major purposes emerge in the literature familiar to
organizational members: 1) separatism as withdrawal to
heal, define or develop, 2) separatism as power-taking,
and 3) separatism as an act of connection.

For the most part, the ideas of separatism as
withdrawal or power-taking are meanings assigned to the
separatist act retrospectively. They may be seen as
accomplishments of the act, but seldom are they the
reasons separatism occurs initially. They are both
relevant to this study because they both emerge in the
sense-making of organizational members. Separatism as

power-taking is considered in Chapter Five in a
discussion of how organizational members perceive
themselves as political, and separatism as withdrawal
is treated in the discussion of the cultural nature of
separatism in this organization later in this chapter.

Jo Freeeman, in The Politics of Women's
Liberation, says that within the women's movement
"lesbianism (has become) redefined to mean much more
than merely sleeping with another woman. It (has)
developed into a worldview which (says) that women
should identify with, live with, and associate only
with women."[9] The primary impetus for the enactment of
this worldview is not power-taking or withdrawal but
the ideas of connection, bonding, or sisterhood - the
fellowship of other women with similarities in
lifestyle and politics.

Alix Dobkin, a radical separatist performer, who
appears exclusively before women-only groups, regards
separatism as a means of "bonding and skill building"
which she sees as the "keys to survival."[10] The need
for this bonding among women is evident, Dobkin
contends, in the "way we (separatist women) are still
measured by the absence of men."[11]

The focus of this worldview concept can be
regarded as more positive than some other
conceptualizations of separatism because it is defined
in terms of women rather than men. It does not overtly
involve the denial of access to men or the withdrawal
from patriarchal pain articulated in the other reasons
for separatism, but is tied to the idea of withdrawal
to develop, both individually and collectively. It is
not antimale, but profemale. Within this worldview the
concepts of separatism and sisterhood are inextricably
woven together. Women-only activities or spaces are

"connections." Women separate to connect.

Most relevant to a discussion of the organization's goals is the conceptualization of separatism as an act of connection. The first claim I will make concerning the characteristic of separatism as enacted in Twenty Rue Jacob is that the primary goal of the organization was to serve a function which could be regarded as separatist in nature - that of providing a "place for women." Alex articulates this goal in talking about the founding of the walk-in business. "We looked at each other and decided there was absolutely nothing more we could offer this community than a place for women to meet, to share, to believe in one another."[12]

This goal is shared by organizational members and articulated in the interaction. "It is so good to come down here and be in women's space." "What would we do without the Rue, it's a place to be together." "I feel so alive when I leave here, all the good woman energy!"

What Alex is talking about when she designates the Rue as a "place for women" is more than the simple provision of physical space. She is also talking about providing connections, a sense of belonging with people who share a similar worldview.

This organizational goal of providing a separate place for women is evident in two enduring organizational symbols: 1) the business name, and 2) the definition and maintenance of specific activities as a separatist ritual.

The business name, Twenty Rue Jacob, adopted by the three initial owners and retained throughout the organization's existence, was the Parisian address of Natalie Clifford Barney, a French lesbian whose "colorful reputation and dozens of affairs" were the

talk of Paris in the early 1900s. Biographer Linda
Simon says that Barney's Academie des Femmes was
conceived as a female counterpart to the all-male
French Academy. It was separatist in that it was
exclusively female. Among the French and American
writers who frequented her salon were Gertrude Stein
and Alice B. Toklas, the poetess Renee Vivien, artist
Romaine Brooks, and writer Elizabeth de Gramont. This
group of lesbian artists and writers, in separating
themselves formed a support group of sisterhood for
women who would otherwise have been isolated in
Parisian society.[13]

In discussing this choice of a name, Alex said:

> Lord only knows the names that we came
> up with - Lavender Menace, like the Purple
> Parrot, like The Iris, like A Woman's Place.
> . . then during one of our meetings Mary
> brought a book, the Judy Chicago book - The
> Dinner Party - she said 'You have to hear
> this, you have to' and she read us a clipping
> out of it which had to do with Natalie
> Clifford Barney. . .[14]

In selecting a name the owners were also seeking a
reflection of their place in the community providing
for the women of Salt lake as Barney had done for the
women of Paris. This is enacted in a separatist ritual
patterned after Barney's gatherings. "Women-only"
activities usually scheduled on Friday evenings, serve
as a means of connecting with other women.

Separatism is maintained in this ritual by means
of a public announcement of the activity's limitation
as women-only space. Both posters hung in prominent

places in the bookstore and announcements in the Women
Aware newsletter explicitly state the separatist nature
of the activity. The fact that the activities take
place during the evening after the business has closed
eliminates the possibility of men wandering in
unintentionally.

There are nonseparatist activities, such as a
combined party with the Lesbian and Gay Student Union
at the university or an autograph party for an author
who spoke at the women's conference at the university,
but the majority of Friday night activities remain
exclusively separatist. The ritual is even a primary
factor in any reconsideration of clientele.
Discussions of change are often amended with a
reaffirmation of Friday nights as 'women-only' space.

Inasmuch as a primary goal of the organization is
to provide a 'separate place,' the second claim I will
make concerns the nature of the 'place' that the Rue
provides.

Separatism as Cultural Nationalism

Lucia Valeska, in an assessment of female
separatism, discusses separatist ideas as occurring
along a continuum. She places cultural nationalists at
one end and political lesbian feminists at the other,
with the qualification that no single individual or
organization exhibits all the characteristics of one,
but rather a general orientation toward one or the
other. Both, she says, "advocate separation of the
sexes organizationally, politically and personally
insofar as separation is possible."[15] The labels, she
says, only represent emerging constellations and she
uses them as a way of elaborating on the range of
lesbian separatist ideas.

Cultural nationalists, Valeska says, speak of revolution in terms of a return of women to the power they held under early matriarchal societies. This is to be accomplished, for now at least, by an emphasis on the creation of a powerful female culture with all the necessary components: music, art, poetry, film, religion, science and medicine. They tend to be antiauthoritarian but not necessarily antimale. Some may consider themselves separatists, but others would not. Cultural nationalists speak of matriarchal revolution with separatism as a strategy for reorganizing society uner a "truly just, fair, loving and creative order." They are primarily content to treat men with a 'live and let live' philosophy, but while they are not usually hostile, their general attitude is that males are "irresponsible and not to be trusted with any degree of power."[16]

Political feminists are at the other end of the continuum. They emphasize rather than discount political analysis, power and structure. Men are the oppressor and relationships with them amount to cooptation. They are generally openly hostile but are interested in grabbing the power back rather than changing the power base. Both groups, however, emphasize the development of collective organizational structures and institutional economic independence and both conceive of this as essential to the feminist revolution. "Taking ground" is a common military strategy. For the lesbian feminist, engaged in a revolution, the act of building a separate, independent, collective territory (geographic, economic, political and sexual) is a strategy of revolution.

The second claim I want to make about the

enactment of separatism in this organization is that it
is essentially cultural; that is, the ways in which
separatism manifests itself communicatively focuses on
the establishment of a strong female culture. I do not
mean, however, that it is apolitical,[17] but rather
that there is a general orientation toward a cultural
emphasis and away from conscious political effort even
though political ideas are still very evident in the
organization's enactment of ideology. Admittedly, it
is very difficult to separate the cultural from the
political aspects in feminist effort. The establishment of a female-based culture is conceptualized as a
political move. Robin Morgan, for example, sees
culture and politics as inseparable aspects of
revolution. "A political revolution that does not take
seriously its artists, and does not see the aesthetic
vision as inseparable in integrity from all political
action, is by definition, a patriarchal revolution."[18]
Thus in terms of Valeska's continuum, the enactment of
separatism in this business can be characterized as
consistent with the ideas reflective of cultural
nationalism

Among lesbians in general, Valeska claims,
cultural nationalism is more evident now, replacing the
early initial militant separatism.

> The army of lovers have set aside
> their spears to make music, poetry, radio
> networks, bookstores, schools, credit unions,
> presses, magazines, farms, cooperatives,
> novels, political theory, health care centers
> and record companies.[19]

This is exemplified in the changes in activity that

have occurred in the Rue over the last few years. The
establishment of the book business of Hon Enterprises
began as a cultural effort. Alex makes note of that
when she says that the main reason she wanted to start
the business was that lesbian and radical feminist
books were "real difficult to get in this city."
Later, when the format changed to that of a walk-in
business, the primary emphasis was still cultural.
This is reflected in the nature of the separatist
activities which, even from the beginning have
emphasized music, art, education, religion and social
development. There was, however, at the beginning more
of a political orientation. Early activities involved
meetings of a group called Political Lesbians whose
efforts, along with those of several other local
women's groups, resulted in the "Take Back the Night"
anti-rape campaign in 1980. Efforts now are more
likely to involve the recently established food co-op
or the sponsorship of a booth selling fruit kabobs at
the Salt Lake Arts Festival.

Occasionally, suggestions are made to increase the
political nature of separatist activities, but even
thesehave cultural rather than political motivations.

> A few years ago there was this group,
> Political Lesbians. We helped sponsor the
> Take Back the Night thing. But that was the
> warmest, most intimate time. We felt so
> together, so close, unified. Issues can
> really bring women together.[20]

The idea of cultural separatism is often articulated by feminist theorists in terms of 'reasons to
separate.' These reasons are directly related to the

nature of the separatist enactment in the organization.

Some regard separatism as a withdrawal from the pain of oppression with the purposes being to define self, establish objectives and to develop theory. The idea of withdrawal for the purpose of theory development was evident in the early years of the contemporary women's movement. Separatist groups were formed by radical feminists in the early 1970s for the purposes of developing a theoretical framework for a feminist revolution and developing alternative institutions embodying feminist ideals.

This reason is evident in the enactment of separatism at Twenty Rue Jacob in the nature of the business itself. At one meeting, a collective member voiced her interests in becoming involved in the organization in the first place when she said that for many of the collective members, getting involved in the Rue was an alternative to working in a traditional system that was seen as oppressive. "We wanted an alternative feminist type business to be part of." The formation of the collective tested the concept of egalitarianism in the workplace. It provided a means to see feminist ideas in action and addressed the issues of hierarchy and decision-making in the workplace.

Withdrawal for self-development and self-definition is also mentioned in separatist literature. Ann Waters regards separatism as a means by which women can better understand the forces of their oppression.

> Just as when a woman is being battered
> she is helped by withdrawal from the
> situation, we who want to preserve and

further women's values must retreat from the
violence and abuse of male culture so that we
can heal and define ourselves.[21]

Marilyn Frye talks about the separation as an
"instinctive and self-preserving recoil from the
systematic misogyny that surrounds us."[22] Similarly
Ti-Grace Atkinson suggests that women "should give more
attention. . . to (their) vulnerability to assault and
degradation, and to separatism as protection."[23]

In the Rue this reasoning is evident in the nature
of activities. Assertiveness training classes, the
planning of a stress management workshop, organized
discussions of relationship issues and single parenting
all were designed to assist women in defining and
developing themselves.

One small intimate Friday evening session resulted
in formation of an ongoing support group for survivors
of sexual child abuse. The activity, announced as the
sharing by three women of "their stories of childhood
abuse, how it has affected their lives and how they
feel as adults about their past," reflects the idea of
separation as withdrawal to heal.

The central idea in all these reasons for
withdrawal is that only within a 'safe' woman-created
space can women discern what they have absorbed from
male-dominated culture and sort through it. Betty
Tallen echoes this idea in her historical analysis of
separatism when she defines it as an "expression of
individual self-worth, empowerment and a reasonable
response to systematic oppression."[24]

Some activities are primarily educational in
nature, such as a session with a lesbian lawyer about
the rights of lesbian couples, classes in stained glass

art, or discussions that focus on topics such as the
healing power of herbs or the feminization of poverty.
Other activities provide a reference group for women
with special interests, such as a lesbian mothers group
or an over-thirties group playfully referred to as OWLS
(older, wiser lesbians).

Incorporated into the idea of withdrawal for
development is the recognition of the creative energies
of women and the encouragement to separate to develop
creative potential. Robin Morgan identifies what she
refers to as the new women's renaissance - an
"explosion of sensibility, creativity, accessibility,
complexity, exploration, philosophy, and arts" as the
releasing of creative female energy previously
suppressed by patriarchal institutions.[25] This
artistic expressive aspect of separatism is defined as
"the expression of women's experiences, ideals and
goals for themselves and the world," by Ruth Iskin, a
founder of two woman-oriented artistic endeavors,
Womanspace and the Los Angeles Women's Building.[26]

The assumption is that women have been oppressed
so long that they must first be encouraged to express
themselves to piece together their existence. That
expression, Iskin says, can be likened to a traditional
women's art form - the quilt.

> The way women have pieced together small
> parts to create a whole has been likened to
> the way women's lives are a structure made up
> of many fragments and interruptions.[27]

This piecing together of women's existence is made
easier, Iskin asserts, by the fact that women are more
often relationship-oriented which has provided them

with easy access to their emotional lives, an important
source for artistic creation.

It is not accidental that much of women's
culture focuses on autobiographical aspects,
renders personal expressions, and uses
collaboration and participation as a
foundation for the artisitic process.[28]

The emphasis on personal expression and creative
participation is evident in many Rue activities. There
is a strong commitment to women-effort. Local artists
are encouraged to place their work on consignment in
the business and occasionally they are invited to hold
special showings. A handicapped woman artist has an
annual showing of her oils, many of them self-
portraits. Two potters and a jeweler combine efforts
and host a Christmas show every December at which wine
and cheese are served. In addition, the Rue has
focused on the works of a local stained glass artist,
two weavers, black and white sketches by one artist,
oils by another. Batik T-shirts and silk-screened
cards are available in the store, and one artist
created a limited edition of sixteen posters with
Twenty Rue Jacob silk-screened across the bottom and
donated the proceeds to the business. The posters sold
within two weeks.

Personal expression and participation are also
encouraged in separatist activities. An example of
this is an art show and poetry reading held one Friday
evening. The following two-page description of the
event provides a means of studying the principles in
action.

Women began arriving a little before 7:00, but it was nearly 7:30 by the time things got under way. The scheduled activity was advertised as an "Open Mike Poetry and Photography Show. . " "Come share your poetry with the rest of us. There will also be 'Women Photos,' by Alex" the ad in the <u>Women Aware</u> newsletter had read. People milled around the room greeting one another with hugs and laughter and studying the carefully matted photos on the walls.

The photos, primarily black and white, were nudes. Some of the women were identifiable, others were not; some were present, others had not attended. The photos, while they might have been termed erotic, were well done and obviously in praise of the female form. The viewers were impressed and studied each photo carefully. Several approached Alex, who was busily rushing about fixing drinks and preparing nachos, with comments of praise.

By 7:30, about twenty-five women had arrived and claimed seats either in the booths or on individual chairs set around the room. Some sat and nervously held pieces of paper or thumbed through notebooks of poetry.

Alex got up and spoke for a few moments about her photos, the philosophy behind her work and the women who had modeled for her. A few women asked questions.

Ann, a local musician, was the first to share her poetry with the group. When Alex called for the first volunteer, Ann hesitated, then hopped up and claimed a stool at the counter. Her work centered on the efforts of composition and her life as a musician. Everyone had words of encouragement and praise. After Ann there was a steady stream of volunteers with an occasional moment of hesitancy. Sometimes a woman needed extra encouragement – some sat on the stool, others stood behind the counter, some staying in their seat.

Some of the poetry was particularly well-written, others were more in the form of a few jumbled thoughts, but everyone received encouragement from the audience. About 9:00 a short break was called and people used the bathroom or got a drink or went outside to smoke a cigarette. (The Rue has a no smoking policy.) The poetry reading did not end until it was clear that everyone had had a chance to read and comment on their work.

When it was over most women participated in helping to clean up and put the extra chairs back in the women's room where they are stored. Most hung around and visited awhile, some car pooled or made plans to meet at the women's bar.

First, as is common of this type of activity, supportiveness takes precedence over critical analysis. Everyone's work was encouraged and praised regardless of its quality. The emphasis was not on making the women "better poets," but on getting them to express themselves creatively and giving them the confidence to share that creativity with others. The focus was the effort rather than the product. The assumption here is that women have been discouraged from even participating in creative effort and that the first hurdle to overcome is their problems with self-worth. Every effort is equally valuable from this frame of reference.

The need for this avenue of creative expression is evident in the attendance. That twenty-five women showed up to participate in a fairly threatening experience attests to this need. Many Friday evening events have a much lower attendance. Furthermore, many

women were very hesitant at first. The supportive
atmosphere bolstered their confidence and the need to
share was more easily realized.

Second, not only was the atmosphere supportive,
but everyone had equal opportunity for participation.
The event would not have ended until everyone who
wanted to had been given an opportunity to participate,
and participate as much as they wanted. Some women
read a single poem, others read several. The structure
of the event was predicated on the needs of the
individual women who had attended. Participation and
reinforcement are evident characteristics in most Rue
events that emphasize women's creative efforts.

There is also an emphasis on the support of women
in business. Conscious efforts at patronizing feminist
professionals and tradespeople and formulating a network of local feminist-oriented organizations is
regarded as a means of shifting the economic base and
providing support for other women. Copies of The
Index, a local guide to women's services and women
professionals, is prominently displayed in the
bookstore.

As is characteristic of feminist businesses, the
owners deal with women whenever possible. A portion of
the Rue bulletin board is devoted to the business cards
of feminist professional women or organizations. It is
not uncommon for women to call or stop in and ask for
help in locating a lawyer, doctor, printer or mechanic.
It is a standing joke that there are no female
gynecologists in private practice in Salt Lake City,
and several times I heard a request for a doctor
responded to with "As long as you don't need a
gynecologist."

While most suppliers the Rue deals with are not
women, much of the repair work on the building is
either done by the women themselves or local women are
hired to do the job. The sagging floor was reinforced
by women and a new water heater was installed by women.
Whenever something is needed the possibility of
utilizing community resources and hiring a woman in
entertained first.

Jane: I wonder if we could buy through a
contractor?

Anne: We should be able to, we wouldn't have to
pay tax that way.

Jane: Do we know any women who do contracting?

Mary: I know there are a bunch of women, but I
don't know who they are.

Anne: Yes, uh, Karen of Joan and Karen - I don't
know her last name.

Mary: Oh, Karen Allen.

Anne: Allen, yeah, she works for um.[29]

*　　*　　*　　*　　*　　*　　*　　*　　*　　*

Cathy: I remember when my sister looked at the
ones (lights) in the back - she said it was
so Mickey Mouse. . . maybe. . . we might be
able to work something out through my
sister - she's an electrician.

Anne: See what you can do for us. . .

Cathy: I think I could talk her into it. . . maybe
even for free.

Anne: or - maybe we could feed her every day for
lunch.

Cathy: She loves to eat.[30]

There is little hesitancy in dealing with male-
dominated companies when it is clear that that is the

only option available and when their services are peripheral to the running of the business. The Pepsi deliveryman delivers only Pepsi to the back door, the Frito Lay deliveryman and the UPS man come in the front. They pose little problem, but entertaining the adoption of a Small Business Administration program was seen as a possible problem.

The differences in the separatist perspective of collective members are evident in this discussion:

Alice: Can I just take five minutes and do the small business consulting? Does everybody agree, do we feel comfortable having a man come in and give us consulting on our business - even though it's free?

Sue: Can I just say something? We don't even know what form their consulting is going to take yet. We don't even know if a man's gonna come in and do some stuff. We don't know if they're gonna give us some books or pamphlets or guidelines or whatever yet.

Jane: This is this university project, right?

Sue: I think it's wise to check it out and see what form the consulting's goin' to take and I agree with doing that. Then we need to talk about what it is they'll wanna do and see whether it's something we want. (pause) I mean that's the process a client goes through when they're dealing with a consultant.

Alice: I know, I know.

Sue: I feel comfortable doing that.

Alice: Well, we need to call and get this initiated. I would like to be the contact person. I'll call and make an appointment

```
                with this guy. . because I'm interested.
                So if everybody agrees?
        Sue:    OK, do it.
        Jane:   Sounds good.31
```

The question entertained here is not so much what form separatism will take, but whether it will be enacted at all. From a radical separatist position allowing a male business consultant amounts to asking the patriarchy for advice. That the question as to whether to do something so radical as to allow a male business consultant access to the business even comes up at all clues us to the tentative and sporadic nature of separatist enactment in the organization. The qualifying factor here is the services that this particular male could offer. The assumption operating behind Sue's insistence on investigating the issue is that man know how to do capitalism, so if that's what we're trying to do here, let's pick up some tricks.

Although it may be attributable to the end of the collective several months later, it is interesting to note that the SBA program was never investigated further.

In conclusion, the objective of the enactment of separatism in this organization is the establishment of a new reality, free of patriarchal oppression. This new reality is seen as possible through the establishment of a strong women's culture which can only be accomplished if women separate themselves to define and develop. Mary Daly regards separatism as a "system of theory of psychological, emotional and physical well-being for women."32 From Daly's perspective this consists of paring away the layers of false selves from the self - the freeing of oneself

from the false identities women have assumed under a
patriarchal system. This is the final objective of Rue
activities. One collective member voiced that when she
said:

> No, we'll never get rid of the women-only
> activities. Women need that. They need it
> to heal and grow and to explore all those
> things that being with other women means.[33]

Having discussed the cultural nature of the enactment of separatism, I now want to address the third
claim: that this cultural separatist nature is
inconsistent with a business definition of the Rue.[34]
Basically what this means is that it is difficult to
establish a separate space in which to define, develop
and establish a women's culture when not enough women
support the efforts to make it a viable business
entity.

Dilemma: Tensions Between Theory and Practice

The enactment of separatism in the organization
becomes problematic in what I will call the separatist/
capitalist dilemma. Here, the contradictions between
'being a business' and 'being separatist' are most
evident and organizational members compensate for that
by developing strategies to deal with the tension.
This dilemma emerges clearly in the problem of defining
the organization's clientele.

For the business to survive it needs the support
of a community. The women's community does not provide
enough support to sustain the business. Only a small
minority patronize the Rue with any regularity. To
make it even more difficult, women usually have less
money than men. Therefore, to survive, either more

women in the community need to begin using the business
or the definition of who constitutes the potential
clientele needs to be reworked.

Attempts to increase patronage among women have
all met with minimal success. These efforts have
included book sales, specials, advertising, and coupons
for free food with a book purchase.

There are specific times when business is
characterized as particularly 'good' or particularly
'bad.' As is the case with business in general,
Christmas is a 'good' time. Extra merchandise is
ordered in anticipation and if additional merchandise
is going to be added it is done then. (For example,
incense was added to the inventory this past
Christmas.) Summer business is characterized as 'bad'
and explanations are similar to explanations one might
typically expect from other businesses: people want to
spend time outside, they are on vacation, etc. Friday
evening activities are suspended and little if any new
merchandise is ordered.

Organizational members, when asked, usually define
their clientele as the Salt Lake women's community.
However, when business problems are being confronted or
lack of support is explicit in the interaction, then
strategies are developed for explaining things.

Alex uses one such strategy by explaining
fluctuations in business in terms of uncontrollable
community-related phenomena. "People aren't coming in
because they think we're too political," or "Everyone's
down on Carol (the owner of a local women's bar) so
they're coming in here now," or "Business has been good
this month because everyone is going through 'annual
bar burn-out,"[35] or "Because several of the collective
members have a lot of education, people think we're

elitist," are typical explanations. These explanations
are usually accompanied by a story which supports or
verifies the contention.

These explanations of phases allow for the
uncertainty that exists because they usually address
the temporary nature of the situation and cannot be
proved inaccurate calling for new explanations later
when 'good' business turns 'bad' or 'bad' business
improves.

On the other hand, explanations of day-to-day
business fluctuations were not as carefully
constructed, perhaps because day-to-day unreliability
was not as threatening as trends which were noted month
to month. Regardless of who made the comment, "I
wonder what kind of day it will be?" The answer was
always "Who knows," often accompanied by a shrug of the
shoulders. For a while, Thursdays were exceptionally
busy, but even that could not be counted on.

> I guess yesterday was a departure from the
> last few Thursdays - only $9 business. It
> never fails, whenever Melanie is here it gets
> real busy - I guess she has been super busy
> the last few Thursdays.[36]

One volunteer had the perception that every second
Friday when people got paid was real busy, but I never
was able to see that. Receipts and the number of
people that came in seemed as unreliable to me on those
as any other days.

There is little relationship between the number of
women that come in and the cash receipts. Thirty women
might be in and out during the day and order only
coffee or five could come in for lunch and buy a couple

of books or records and bring in the same money. More
than once I heard a comment similar to this one:

> If every woman in the community (meaning
> lesbian community) would come in here and
> have lunch or buy a book even once a month -
> we'd be doing great.

There is no way to obtain accurate statistics on
the number of lesbians in Salt Lake City who make up
the potential clientele of the bookstore, but there is
the perception among organizational members that the
number of women who come in regularly are only a very
small percentage of the community.[37] Comments that
indicate amazement are very common:

> Scarcely a day goes by that some dyke I never
> saw before comes in here. Do you know those
> women in the bookstore?[38]
> Everytime I go to the bar, I don't know 90%
> of the women in there. Never saw them before
> in my life. I don't know where they come
> from.[39]

Regardless of where they come from, there is some
surety of where they do not go, at least on any regular
basis, and that is Twenty Rue Jacob, and that is a
source of some pain and frustration for organizational
members. A general feeling of 'where are they?' (the
customers) pervades many business days. The Salt Lake
lesbian community is described as "fickle" or
"politically unaware" and there is often a bitter note
in efforts to do things.

It bugs me a lot, people expect this place to
cater to their needs. I get the impression
that they feel they can come in here and be
relaxed and uh, interact with one another on
a freer level - and yet they don't expect to
want to pay anything for that, like they
don't even wanta pay commitment to coming in
here a lot.[40]

Between attempts to bring in more lesbians, there
are attempts at redefinitions of who constitutes the
potential clientele, which is variously described as
lesbians only, feminist women, gay males and lesbians
and anybody who happens in.

Occasionally, particularly around the time of
involvement in the women's conferences at the
university or at the time of the publication of an
article in Ms. which mentioned the bookstore, there is
increased interest in pulling in more feminist women.
Ads are placed in feminist- oriented publications, such
as Network, and a booth at women's conferences stresses
the feminist nature of the business. When nonlesbian
feminists do come in, their presence is greeted with
enthusiasm and hope.

Five women came in today. I saw them coming
and thought, 'Oh no, relief society women.
They don't know where they are.' They
looked like they'd just come from relief
society, but they came in and had lunch and
bought a bunch of books - feminist, not
lesbian.

They seemed real comfortable. I made them
extra special sandwiches, extra chips, the
works.[41]
Carol: That was another woman who read about
us in Ms.
Jill: Great![42]

A more recent and more practical solution to the
money problem emerges in the effort to attract more gay
males. This solution, however, presents a problem in
terms of separatism. The possibility of catering to
the gay male population emerges as one solution to the
money problem. This solution, however, presents a
problem because it clearly violates a separatist ideal.
On the one hand, organizational members often talk
about attracting gay male patrons as if no problem
exists. "We need to get those men in here spending
money." But on the other hand, the positive,
beneficial aspects of the Rue are conceptualized in
women-to-women terms. "The Rue is a space for women."
"There isn't really any other place here where women
can just be with other women."

The understanding of what 'separatism' means in
the organization is elusive. Organizational members
never explicitly discussed what separatism meant for
Twenty Rue Jacob. Shared understanding was minimal and
was negotiated as issues arose within the context of
events to occur or decisions to be made.

Theory and practice were not consistent.
Organizational members might say "I'm not a separatist
anymore," or "We can't afford to be separatist," but
when men came in, particularly men who were not
perceived as gay, conversation usually ceased and the
atmosphere became tense until they left. Sometimes the

uncomfortable quiet would be broken with a comment
after they were gone, such as "and don't come back."
This was not always the case and depended on several
factors, such as the nature of the conversation that
was interrupted and who happened to be there when they
arrived. In general, though, male presence was usually
regarded as intrusive. But there was enough confusion
and enough inconsistency to make it next to impossible
to decide who 'should' be there and who 'should not.'

This confusion is evident in this conversation
that occurred between three women who were involved in
redecorating the coffeehouse during the summer of 1983.
The three were painting and discussing plans for the
changing image of the business:

Alice: Where's the vacuum and I'll clean up
     this stuff?

Susan: It's in the 'other.'

Alice: If we're goin' ta try to attract some
     of the men we're going to have to
     change that - ya know? If I was a
     woman and went into a male bar - and
     the sign on the women's room said
     'other' I'd be offended.

Susan: Ann has made some jewelry for men -
     and we're goin' get some books for
     men.

Janet: (surprised) So, are we goin' to try to
     attract the men? (everyone laughs) I
     mean, I think. . .

Susan: Phoenix has one bathroom and a
     women/men sign - you can just flip it.

Alice: When those friends of Alex's came in
     they wanted jewelry made, a lambda, I
     think - then a woman came in later and

asked to have some made for male
friends.

Susan: Well, they're over 50% of the
population and have well over 50% of
the money. . .

Alice: so business wise. . .

Susan: Yeah, we're cutting our own throats.

Alice: As long as we keep Friday nights
'women only' and I think the men will
understand that. . .It's a tradition -
they're into tradition - they have
their own.

Susan: Some of them are really nice - like
that retired English professor from
BYU - he came in once with his
lover.[43]

Several things are going on here to make the
impending changes (the practice) appear consistent with
the ideals (the theory) of organizational members.
This is done in terms of explanations and justifications and by redefining separatism. There is an effort
here to reconceptualize separatism, or the manifestation of separatism in the Friday night ritual as
'tradition.' This reconceptualization, talking about
separatist activities as ritual or at least the
suggestion that they might be explained that way to the
men, allows one to transcend the separatist/capitalist
dilemma.

This example suggests that redefinition is working
at two levels. The changes occurring at the event
level are explicit. The sign on the bathroom door,
"others," has to be changed and new books and jewelry
have been ordered. The changes at the individual level

are harder in coming and still need justification and
qualification.

"They're over 50% of the population and have well
over 50% of the money" addresses the capitalist in the
speakers, the implication being that this is a business
and it is here to make money. Hanging on to a strict
separatist definition proves to be at odds with a
'business' definition of the Rue. So the speaker
redefines the Rue, too. The Rue here is not an enactment of feminism, it is a business and so, in redefining just what separatism means, what the women seem to
be doing is approaching it from a 'business' standpoint
to make it okay, and reconceptualizing it from a male
definition. By calling it tradition and recognizing it
as a cultural ritual, it becomes acceptable to gay male
patrons since they have 'traditions' too. The only way
this would ever be done is on a business level, they
reconceptualize the ideology, at least appear to
reconceptualize it, to survive.

What Susan does in bringing up the bathroom sign
at Phoenix is not suggest an alternative solution for
the Rue, because this solution does not meet the
criteria anyway. The Rue has two bathrooms, not the
one bathroom problem that their sign is a solution to.
What is being accomplished is an understanding that not
being strictly separatist is okay. Phoenix is feminist
and it is not separatist so maybe it is okay.

A similar discussion occurred at a collective
meeting when a proposal was presented by one woman, who
later became an owner, to open the business as an
after-bar breakfast place on weekends. The extra money
it would bring outweighs any ideological considerations.

Jane: My only concern was, when she said it first, was 'Oh great, we're tryin' to clean up our act to have a more, nice image and we're gonna do this thing! But then I thought about it and well, it's a completely different time of day, the people aren't gonna interface with our other customers, our book buying customers and, uh, ya know, so I was able to deal with it.

Ann: It sounds like maybe we should beef up our gay men's selection.

Lynn: Then maybe they'll come back in during the week to buy books.

Jane: That's what we're thinking, that's what we're talking about, that's what we're hoping and that's why, if we can make it look nice they'll wanna come back.

Meg: Yeah, we need to open ourselves to gay men.

Ann: Two came in yesterday and said, 'Oh, you have our favorite table,' like they come in there all the time. I was sitting by the window.

Mary: Well, you missed the guy that came in in chains all over his body who wanted to know if Jane knew any women who were really into reading the Bible. (laughter)

Jane: You wanna hear the worst part? I go 'No, I don't know any women who are really inta that..and the women who come in here wouldn't be interested.'

> Than I had my back to him, I was at
> the cash register, and he moved and I
> swear I jumped a mile. I just finally
> said, 'Hey, I really don't like your
> energy.'

Ann: You said that?

Jane: Yeah, and ya know what he said - 'I'm
not surprised, you shouldn't.'[44]

In this example, the dilemma is made explicit. Even though the after-bar crowd, which was most likely to be heavily male, would not interface with the daily customers, there was nonetheless enthusiasm about them returning during the day to have lunch or buy books. The concern is more with the rowdiness of an after-bar crowd than with the gender of the people coming through the door.

Even with the recognition of the 'need' to cater to gay males, there is still some confusion as to what it will mean if men begin to come in regularly. Mary, in bringing up the example of the guy in chains makes that confusion explicit.

If confusion is evident among the owners, it is even more evident in conversations with some customers. This next example occurred on a day that I was volunteering. Cindy and I were behind the counter. Tom, the only regular male was sitting in a booth and having a cup of coffee while he reads his paper. A couple of women were sitting around the room. A woman walked in and ordered coffee, sat quietly at the counter. Tom paid for his coffee and left.

Customer: What was he doing in here?

Cindy:	Having a cup of coffee and reading his paper. (pause) He comes in a lot.
Customer:	Oh, I thought this was a woman's place.
Cindy:	It is.
Customer:	Oh, I thought maybe things had changed. (shrugs shoulders)[45]

This customer addresses the dilemma. If this is a woman's space, then why is a man in here? It becomes obvious to her that there is some knowledge she does not share. Apparently, this separatism thing is more complex than she thought. She is working from the assumption that separatism has a radical separatist definition in this business, that men are not allowed or at least not welcome. The fact that Tom is there at all confuses her, but the fact that Cindy seems calm about that fact confuses her even more. Presence she can explain: he might have stumbled in and Cindy not asserted herself to let him know the rules, or he might be gay and waiting for a friend, but acceptance she cannot understand. She anticipates a different response from Cindy than she gets - at the very least - a negative one. "I don't know, the jerk was probably checkin us all out," would have encompassed her understanding of the separatist aspects of the business, but a straightforward description of his activities does not. It becomes obvious that she is dealing with knowledge she does not possess so, rather than pursue it, she backs off.

This confusion is even more evident among gay males. The following conversation occurred about lunch time after one collective member had just answered the phone:

> Lynn: You'll never believe this! You'll
> never believe. (laughing hysterically)
>
> Cindy: What? What?
>
> Lynn: That was Allen on the phone!
>
> Cindy: Yeah?
>
> Lynn: He called to ask permission to come
> down for lunch.
>
> Cindy: What?
>
> Lynn: He said, "I was wondering, ah, is it
> all right if I come down for lunch
> today?'
>
> Cindy: (with a serious expression) So, what
> did you tell him? (Everyone in the
> place laughs.)[46]

While certainly seldom this explicit, the
confusion is obvious because the reputation of the
bookstore is decidedly separatist - it is referred to
by gay males as a 'lesbian place.' One gay male said
to me, "Isn't that the lesbian place?" Another came in
and jokingly said, "Excuse me, is this the Lebanese
bookstore?"

This confusion then, between separatism and capitalism, prevents the organization from establishing a
clear direction, because at the same time it is trying
to satisfy the goal of providing a 'separate' place for
women, it is trying to become a successful business
entity. The organization is locked into pursuing what
is for them cross purposes. To survive as a business,
it must sacrifice or at least reconcep- tualize the
ideology; while to serve the purposes of the ideology,
it must somehow limit the clientele. Neither course of
action seems viable, or at least viable enough for

organizational members to commit themselves to one
course of action to the exclusion of the other.

Conclusions

It seems unrealistic to declare separatism a dead
issue for feminists. As Lucia Valeska says in talking
about the contradictions between theory and practice,
"It is somewhat bizarre to be pronounced dead on
arrival when your eyes are wide open and your blood is
running hot."[47] It seems unlikely that separatism will
die out, but the nature of that separatism is changing
in practice. In this organization, it is becoming more
cultural, more symbolic and perhaps more practical and
workable to allow the business to survive. At the same
time, this redefinition is taking its toll on the
reasons for separatism in the first place.

In an interview with Robin Morgan on the definition of women's culture, Gayle Kimball asked about the
role of men in women's culture and the nature of
separatism. Morgan's response echoes the direction
that separatism seems to be taking in this business.

> I think that there's a period where it's
> separatist (women's culture) and it needs to
> be separatist. . . Even Virginia Woolf said
> that. . .she was nonetheless writing as if
> there were men in the next room overhearing
> her, so she was still writing as if for their
> approval. . . It is necessary that we
> discover and develop our own voices. . . I
> do hope this is a phase, though, mainly
> because I think that what women have to say.
> . . is capable of transforming the entire
> species, and has to. There comes a sort of
> suicidal point if we insist on talking to

ourselves and on leaving outside and
unaffected all those who happen to have
power, money, munitions, material, and the
means of ending the planet. That makes me
nervous.[48]

Sasha Lewis refers to women-only spaces as
"workshops of separatism."[49] This characterization
fits well for Twenty Rue Jacob. As an enactment of
feminist ideology, the organization reflects the same
diversity and confusion and uncertainty, the same
contradictions between theory and practice, that is
evident in the writings of feminists.

CHAPTER 5
ENDNOTES

[1]Sasha Gregory Lewis, Sunday's Women: A Report on Lesbian Life Today (Boston: Beacon Press, 1979), p. 165.

[2]Adrienne Rich, "Notes for a Magazine: What Does Separatism Mean?" Sinister Wisdom, No. 18 (1981), pp. 83-91.

[3]Lucis Valeska, "The Future of Female Separatism," in Building Feminist Theory: Essays From Quest (New York: Longman, Inc., 1981) pp. 20-31.

[4]Marilyn Frye, The Politics of Reality: Essays in Feminist Theory (New York: The Crossing Press, 1983) p. 95.

[5]Marilyn Frye, p. 96.

[6]Marilyn Frye, p. 96.

[7]Karen Mudd, "Lesbian Separatism: Then and Now," Off Our Backs, August/September 1983, p. 10.

[8]Marilyn Frye, p. 96.

[9]Jo Freeman, The Politics of Women's Liberation (New York: Longman, 1975).

[10]Karen Mudd, p. 10.

[11]Karen Mudd, p. 10.

[12]History Tape (5/19/83).

[13]Linda Simon, The Biography of Alice B. Toklas (New York: Avon Books, 1978) p. 160.

[14]History Tape (5/19/83).

[15]Lucia Valeska, p. 22.

[16]Lucia Valeska, p. 23.

[17]Organizational participants regard even their existence to be a radical political act. This idea is explored in detail in Chapter 5.

[18]"Defining Women's Culture: An Interview with Robin Morgan," in Women's Culture: The Women's Renaissance of the Seventies ed. by Gayle Kimball (Boston: The Scarecrow Press, Inc., 1981) p. 30.

[19]Lucia Valeska, p. 25.

[20]Conversation at an OWL (Older, Wiser Lesbians) Meeting held in the Rue (11/17/83).

[21]Karen Mudd, p. 10.

[22]Marilyn Frye, p. 97.

[23]Marilyn Frye, p. 97, footnote.

[24]Karen Mudd, p. 10.

[25]Gayle Kimball with Robin Morgan, p. 31.

[26]"Institutions of Women's Culture: Interview with Ruth Iskin," in Women's Culture: The Women's Renaissance of the Seventies ed. by Gayle Kimball (Boston: The Scarecrow Press, 1981) p. 280.

[27]Gayle Kimball with Ruth Iskin, p. 288.

[28]Gayle Kimball with Ruth Iskin, p. 288.

[29]Discussion at a collective retreat - Windsor Street House (5/11/83).

[30]Discussion at a collective retreat - Windsor Street House (5/11/83).

[31]Discussion at a collective retreat - Windsor Street House (5/11/83).

[32]Mary Daly, Gyn/Ecology: The Metaethics of Radical Feminism (Boston: Beacon Press, 1978) pp. 381-82.

[33]Conversation in the Rue with Alex (4/17/83).

152

[34]This is not to say that 'separatism' and 'business' are always inconsistent concepts, only that in this business in the context in which they are operating they are inconsistent.

[35]Annual 'bar burn-out' is a phenomenon that seems to be used to explain just about any change in the gay community in general. When Alex told me business had increased because of 'bar burn-out,' I gave her a skeptical look. She countered with "It's true, I've seen it happen again and again."

[36]Observation Notes - Conversation in the Rue (8/25/82).

[37]A statistic which seems to be quoted often among gay people is that a conservative estimate of the gay population is 10% nationally. In Salt Lake this would be approximately 40,000.

[38]Observation Notes - Conversation in the Rue (1/7/83).

[39]Observation Notes - Conversation in the Rue (4/10/83).

[40]Interview with a collective member in the Rue (8/5/83).

[41]Observation Notes - Conversation in the Rue (4/10/83).

[42]Observation Notes - Conversation in the Rue (10/83).

[43]Conversation between three collective members while painting during the summer of '83 (7/83).

[44]Collective Meeting - Windsor Street House (5/11/83).

[45]Observation Notes - Conversation in the Rue (8/22/83).

[46]Observation Notes - Conversation in the Rue (5/12/83).

[47]Lucia Valeska, p. 38.

[48]Gayle Kimball with Robin Morgan, p. 38.

[49]Sasha Gregory Lewis, p. 167.

CHAPTER VI

CONTRADICTION AND CHANGE

In Chapters Three, Four and Five, I examined three ideological components evident in Twenty Rue Jacob that center on the notion of 'community:' sisterhood, politicalism, and separatism. Organizational contradictions emerge in the enactment of each of these components in different ways and to differing degrees.

In sisterhood, the notion of community becomes ideologically defined and contradiction is evident, but manageable. That is, when the meanings assigned to the concept of sisterhood are inconsistent with the meanings assigned to the concept of business, the contradiction can still be lived out in day-to-day organizational life. Unlike politicalism or separatism, the notion of community is manifested in sisterhood primarily on a personal or relationship level. On this level, a synthesis of sisterhood and business is possible by redefining or re-explaining the concepts to make them appear consistent. An example of this is the imposition of a 'family' metaphor on the idea of 'business.' Not only is the metaphor consistent with both concepts, but is not uncommonly applied to business or organizational settings.

In the concept of politicalism, however, contradiction becomes more pronounced. Community becomes
defined in politicalism on a theoretical level. The
meanings assigned to the political nature of things are
more rigid and less easily redefined than in sisterhood. By the assumption of a political nature, both
individually (as lesbians) and collectively (as a
business), organizational members effectively limit the
responses they can formulate to handle contradiction.
'Sisterhood' can 'mean' any number of things--it is
never even explicitly defined in the theoretical
literature, but political has a narrower range of
acceptable meanings within the worldview of organizational members so that when it comes to selecting
organizational responses to problems or resolving
contradictions, there is a limited repertoire of
possible 'correct' choices. Furthermore, members
cannot deny the political nature of the business since
they operate on the assumption that the business is a
political statement. It is manageable primarily
because it exists on a theoretical level even though it
emerges in practice in minor contradictions.

In the concept of separatism, however, community
becomes defined in practice. It is in this enactment
of community that contradiction is the most pronounced,
most problematic and least successfully managed. One
reason for this is that the contradiction at this level
of practice was not explicitly recognized. The goal of
the organization, to provide a place for women, is
essentially a separatist goal. Unfortunately, this
separatist goal proved to be totally inconsistent with
a business definition of this organization. This
creates an almost unresolvable dilemma - members must
redefine the ideology and renegotiate their purpose or

see the business fail. Strategies developed to cope
with this kind of dilemma most often involve avoidance
or compensation rather than strategies to make things
appear consistent. Thus the examination of these three
ideological enactments reveal a major organizational
contradiction between the notion of community, which is
exclusive, and the notion of business, which is non-
exclusive. Organizational members are tied to enacting
both of these mutually exclusive alternatives. The
contradiction emerges clearly in the relationship
between what organizational members say and what they
do.

This dialectical relationship between theory and
practice has been ignored in most organizational
studies. J. Kenneth Benson (1977) says, "Established
perspectives fail to deal with the production of
organizational arrangements or to analyze the entangle-
ment of theories in those arrangements."[1] He proposes
a dialectical approach which focuses on the process by
which organizational arrangements are produced and
maintained. The organization is conceptualized as a
multileveled phenomenon laced with contradictions that
undermine the existing features. The direction of
change depends "upon the interests and ideas of people
and upon their power to produce and maintain a social
formation."[2]

Linda Putnam argues, in a similar vein, that
contradiction and paradox are viable means for understanding subtle as well as dramatic organizational
change. Contradiction, she says, is a natural outgrowth of change. It "evolves from the circumstances
we encounter, i.e., from attempts to cope and adapt to
a continuously changing environment" and in turn it
provides a viable means, or a starting point "for

examining the complexities of messages and meanings as they impact on organizational change.[3] Perhaps, she says, we can "discover how organizations pull themselves out of self-made quagmires by their own bootstraps,"[4] or as is more likely the case here, how it happens that they cannot.

Both Benson and Putnam locate organizational change in the processes of social construction and regard contradiction as the moving factor which regulates the production and maintenance of social formations. It functions as a catalyst for change. For Benson the organization is characterized by "ruptures, breaks, and inconsistencies in the social fabric," to which he applies the general term contradiction while acknowledging that such rifts may be of different types. Putnam, however, delineates several categories or types of rifts. She centers her discussion on the concept of paradox. The term comes from the Greek word para + dokein which means "to think twice; to reconcile two apparently conflicting views."

The rest of this analysis focuses on the responses of organizational members to contradiction since it is response that determines the direction of change. Building on the work of Putnam and Benson, I will 1) discuss the concept of contradiction in terms of the assumptions of the interpretive approach, 2) examine the major location in the organization's enactment where this contradiction emerges, and 3) discuss the responses of organizational members to contradiction in terms of the strategies developed to manage contradictory situations.

Interpretive Assumptions and 'Contradictions'

As was stressed in Chapter Two (p. 8), the interpretive approach reflects the view that reality is
socially constructed through words, symbols, and
behavior. From this perspective reality is defined,
maintained and redefined in the communicative experience of its members. "The social world is in a
continuous state of becoming - social arrangements
which seem fixed and permanent are temporary, arbitrary
patterns and any observed social patterns are regarded
as one among many possibilities.[5] Through communication and organizing, then, individuals construct a
social reality with a stable set of meanings and
arrangements that are altered, modified and sustained
in an ongoing dynamic process. The focus of study in
an examination of contradiction then is on how specific
social arrangements emerge, are challenged and dissolve.

Relevant to this study is the idea of interpretive
schemes that individuals use to make sense of what
others say and mean. These interpretive schemes, or
the meanings we assign to our communicative experience,
emanate from the simultaneous interplay among three
components: 1) message factors, 2) interpretations of
those factors, and 3) the context in which the message
and interpretation occur.[6] A message and interpretation occur in a particular organizational context and
members not only use the context to interpret messages,
but use the messages to change the context. W. B.
Pearce and V. E. Cronon assert that organizational
interpretations form repertoires of stable meanings and
therefore "interpretations of messages and events are
social and cognitive constructions, created through
action within context.[7] Thus, from an interpretive

perspective, communication in an organizational setting can be described as a "continual process of creating and/or reaffirming interpretations through the inter-locked behaviors of organizational members."[8]

Contradictions, then, emerge as a part of this natural process of reality construction, modification and reconstruction, and are seated in the notion that people and messages change over time. This is il-lustrated in the following example:

> It is plausible that an individual who par-ticipates in a women's consciousness raising group will send messages that contradict communication prior to this experience. Her adjustments to changes in herself and in her perceived environment contribute to this duplicity.[9]

Despite the fact that contradiction is part of the natural process of change, we evaluate human behavior in terms of consistency and predictability. Organiza-tions that send contradictory messages or appear inconsistent are regarded as unreliable or direction-less. Yet, contradiction is an inevitable part of change not only in individuals, but in organizations.

This perspective on change as related to contradic-tion and the natural process of social construction provides an alternative to traditional 'rigid' defini-tions of organizational change. Change in organiza-tions is usually talked about in terms of changes in policy, procedure or structure. Aspects of the process of change are regarded as fixed and immediate. Changes take 'time' in organizations because the altering of policies and procedures to bring them in line with the

'new way of doing things' takes time. There is little
room for the ambiguity arising out of change, particularly if it cannot be relegated to 'red tape.' If
one can say, "Oh, I know. That rule hasn't been
changed to make it consistent with the new policy, we
better do that" that makes the contradiction explicit
and change understandable in acceptable terms. A
perspective on change that regards it as a 'natural
process' rather than the implementation of organizational decision-making allows us to see how changes
come about outside of administrative plans.

Contradiction in Twenty Rue Jacob

The type of paradox that has the most relevance in
this study of Twenty Rue Jacob is the pragmatic
paradox. In this paradox, contradictions are mutually
exclusively alternatives that evolve over time. An
example of this can be found in orphanages and welfare
systems. These agencies exist to place homeless
children in 'healthy' home environments, but they often
develop rules and regulations which preclude them from
placing children in many 'excellent' home environments.
In the process of accomplishing their goals, "they
create standard operating procedures that defy their
very aims for existence."[10] Contradictions such as
these are created communicatively by organizational
members as they go about attempting to accomplish their
goals. They evolve over time through interaction.

One specific kind of pragmatic paradox is of
particular use here - the systems contradiction. This
type of contradiction is a result of the struggle
between the "prevailing structure and practices which
run counter to that structure."[11] A systems contradiction emerges when an organization's practices (ways of

getting things done) become incongruent with an organization's structures (rules, procedures, goals and policies for operating). This construction can be applied to the dialectical relationship between theory (ideology) and practice (enactment) in this organization. At Twenty Rue Jacob the organization's business structure was incongruent with the separatist practices which emerged as a result of the organization's ideology. The women of the Rue were "being a business" so that they could meet the goal of providing a "place for women," but these proved to be mutually exclusive contradictory alternatives.

The major location of systems contradiction is in the clash between prevailing objectives, goals, or structures and the constraining effects of these creations, which define the limits of change within a particular period or within a given system. "When created social arrangements become dysfunctional, they are transformed; only to find that the cure for the ill becomes the ill."[12]

One study that has some explanatory power here is David Berg's examination of an all-women public relations firm. This organization was founded on feminist egalitarian values - work was shared and all workers were expected to provide input into group decision-making efforts. However, as the organization grew, a group of elites began to form and exert more influence on the company. The very existence of this elite group, however, was inconsistent with the egalitarian ideology of the organization. The ideology imposed constraints which precluded the possibility of formalizing the emerging informal structure.

Similar systems contradictions emerged in Twenty Rue Jacob in the formation and operation of the collective structure. The formation of the collective was an ideological response to a business problem. Yet its formulation as ideological imposed expectations on the structure that were inconsistent with its formation as a 'business' move. These contradictions emerged in the way 'collective'; was accomplished (practice) more than in features of a collective structure itself (theory).

An example of this is the concept of egalitarianism. Regardless of status or outside obligation, equality was an expectation. The focus in the organization was on the sharing of responsibility, work and reward. Many of the tensions in the structure and perhaps even the failure of the form in this organization may to some extent be attributed to this expectation. When the collective was initially formed there was a shortage of women available for involvement - the criteria focused more on questions of personality, "Can we get along with this person and can they be a successful member of the group?" than on questions regarding their philosophical approach to collectivism. If group members thought an individual would fit in, then the extent of their involvement and their method of payment was, to some extent, negotiable. While all agreed to a commitment, members had differing meanings for commitment. This led to an inequity in involvement. One member joined with the understanding that she would do the minimum but that she had a job outside the business that held higher priority for her. She would make up for her lesser time involvement in other ways which were negotiated, but among the others, some did only the minimum while others spent long hours in the business.

This led to an ambiguous situation. Some members
operated as though 'egalitarianism' meant one thing
(amount of time spent in the business, for example) and
others operated as though it meant another (being here
when I can). As changes occurred and the demands of
the business increased, the negotiated tasks were no
longer needed. Some members had increasing obligations
outside the business and members began to regard the
situation as inequitable. "I'm tired of a few people
doing all the work," or "Where's Alice, shouldn't she
be putting in some time making shish kabobs?"

Some members began criticizing the level and
quality of the involvement of other members, most often
using the feminist principle of egalitarianism as a
measure of their commitment to the business. One
member said:

> . . .that's kinda perplexing - in a way, ya
> know? . . .my hypothesis was the more
> feminist-oriented would see that you need to
> share the work and that isn't generally how
> it worked. . . I still put this first, so
> my priority was different than some of the
> other people. Some of the attitudes were,
> well, ya know, 'You might choose to do this,
> but I choose to do this' and the kinda stuff
> that I think is real bullshit, because I
> guess that's sorta what I had hoped to see
> is people would say, 'Hey, I really would
> like it this way, but I'm gonna sacrifice
> for the good of the total things. . .that's
> part of the problem, is that who judges what
> is going to be equal to what.[13]

They saw arrangements as inequitable in light of the changes that had taken place and attempted to restructure them by asserting their expectations.

This is an example of contradictions emerging from change. At the time of formation the collective was a perfect ideological response to the problem the business was experiencing, but as change occurred, contradiction emerged in the practice which made the collective as enacted appear inconsistent with both the ideology and accomplishing 'business.' It could be let go of because it was not successfully meeting either ideological or business criteria.

Another example of the constraints imposed by the existing system is in the change generated by efforts to enact 'successful business' by attracting a new and different group of clientele. The organization's morphology is the officially enforced and conventionally accepted view of the organization as embodied in the prevailing objective, and goals. Within the ongoing process of social construction, alternatives to this morphology are constantly generated. The nature of these alternatives or 'innovations' are seated in the process of organizing:

> Organizational members create their procedures and policies; these enactments operate for a period of time until they become dysfunctional. Some members then, begin to organize differently - to create new procedures and structures that run counter to the prevailing ones, so that innovations, whether officially sanctioned or not, frequently oppose the prevailing way of 'doing things around here.[14]

Contradictions then, often occasion dislocation and crisis which stimulate the search for alternative arrangements. When innovations clash with the established morphology "the organization as established constitutes a structure which may resist its own further development."[15]

Such was the case in Twenty Rue Jacob. As it became apparent to organizational members that the 'women's community' was not supporting the business, that the current way of doing things was dysfunctional, some members began to talk in terms of innovations. Some of these innovations, efforts to attract more women through advertising, coupons, new activities, etc. were consistent with the organization's morphology. Others, such as attracting gay male customers, were in opposition to the prevailing way of doing things, which was constituted in the organizational goal of providing a "place for women." This aspect of the morphology was resistent to change. It allowed for the entertainment of creative alternatives, but made it difficult for organizational members to implement the alternatives because of the contradictions. Thus, organizational members could paint and redecorate the interior, order new merchandise and talk about redesigning the logo, but even these changes were often limited by the established morphology. For example, the redecorating included the framing of signed women's music posters and the talk of the new logo included women-oriented flower images despite the fact that organizational members talked most often about attracting gay male customers.

Response to Contradiction in Twenty Rue Jacob

Contradictions have the potential to be system integrative or system destructive and whether contradictions emerge as catalysts for change or death knells for organizations is dependent to a great degree on the response of organizational participants.

According to Krippendorf "every system carries in it the seeds of its own destruction."[16] Typically, however, when crises perpetuated by contradiction occur, the organization absorbs the crisis by integrating it into the established order. One method of doing this is by institutionalizing or formalizing contradiction in some way, e.g., legitimating labor conflicts, strikes, technological change. This, however, is most often characteristic of contradictions that do not clash with the dominant organizational ideology. On the other hand, when the status quo resists transformation, contradictions can undermine and destroy the system. When the ideology is one source of contradiction, the options become 1) changing the ideology to accommodate the contradiction or 2) allowing the system to destroy itself.

The process whereby these options are enacted is one focus of this study. In Twenty Rue Jacob, in terms of the nature of the contradictions and the organization's response to them, the most explanatory power is possible by regarding the process that was enacted as system destructive.

Contradiction in Twenty Rue Jacob, then, emerges in the relationship between the established organizational morphology, practices that run counter to it and the constraints it imposes on the system. Organizational members may, for example, go about their day-to-day lives enacting a women's bookstore, catering

to women and planning women's activities, while at the
same time discussing and making changes to attract male
patrons that are limited by the established way of
doing things.

Inconsistencies in organizational practices may
operate together for some time. Dale argues that
individuals are capable of functioning normally within
contradictory situations, but when contradiction
emerges as explicit, the enactment of one aspect of the
contradiction will impinge on and impede the enactment
of the other.17 At this point, according to Zeitz,
contradictions serve as a necessary and sufficient
condition for transforming a system.[18]

Organizational responses to contradiction are not
predetermined. There are any number of ways in which
organizational members can respond when confronted with
inconsistency. The most useful way to talk about
contradiction here is to talk about it in terms of
accomplishment. What does the strategy formulated to
manage the contradiction do for organizational members
and how does it do it? This analysis focuses on three
major organizational responses to contradiction evident
in this business: 1) suppression, 2) dispersion and 3)
repression. These responses are hierarchical in the
sense that each one builds on and leads to another.
They cannot really be regarded as stages, because they
do not operate in a sequential fashion, but the
existence of one may create conditions that call for
the formulation or creation of another to manage the
dilemma created by the first response.

Suppression

Suppression refers to the degree to which organizational members fail to explicitly recognize contradic-

tion in the organization's enactment. This is most evident in contradictions between theory and practice. When Lucia Valeska says that "while many claim to no longer be separatist, they continue to live it" she addresses this duplicity. She tells one story that makes explicit a major contradiction in this organization:

> Recently, three women from Seattle's Radical Women sailed through town on their way home from the Antioch Socialist-Feminist bash. A query on separatism gleaned from them a resounding: 'It's dead in Seattle.' But, they quickly added, 'three-quarters of our membership is lesbian and we're an autonomous female organization.'[19]

What this accomplishes for organizational members is that it allows them to ignore the problems inherent in the contradiction, but it also limits their ability to deal with contradiction or manage its effects, because they are constantly striving to understand what is going on.

We enact organizations and our enactments, in turn, impose on us and limit our behaviors. In Twenty Rue Jacob, the enactment of the organization's ideology imposed limits on the behavior of organizational participants within the context of the business, constraining the nature of change. The communicative responses to contradiction can generate an awareness of the limitations imposed. By entertaining alternatives and reframing events, organizational members can reconstruct the prevailing system in such a way as to overcome limitations. Strategies are developed as a

means of managing existing contradictions that can
provide new insight and help transform the system.
Individuals can transcend their existing social
arrangements through an awareness of their condition
and through changes in their organizing process.
Contradictions then can function as opportunities for
change, but in Twenty Rue Jacob, because they were
often suppressed, they functioned as problems to be
explained and then resolved, strategized and gotten
around. They cannot fully function as opportunities
when they were not explicitly recognized as contradictions.

Dispersion

Contradiction that is not explicitly recognized
cannot, therefore, be successfully managed and tends to
be dispersed throughout the system. Dispersion at the
contradiction refers to the "existence of multiple
inconsistencies across organization events, levels and
boundaries."[20] One way in which this is manifested is
in communication levels.

Putnam contends that the verbal-nonverbal,
literal-metaphorical, abstract-concrete and con-
tent-relationship dichotomies provide fertile ground
for incompatibility in organizations inasmuch as
meaning is derived from an aggregate of different
levels of interaction.[21] In fact, systems contradictions frequently emerge in the organizational enactment
of these different levels. One location of this,
related to the theory-practice dichotomy, is in the
message-action relationship. This is descriptive of
some of what is going on in Twenty Rue Jacob.

When organizational members become quiet or
exchange glances when males come into the business,

post signs for 'womyn only' activities or maintain that
the "Rue is a space for womyn" and then place orders
for male-oriented books and jewelry, a message-action
contradiction emerges. So that, while enacting some
practices to attract gay males, other messages turn
them away, and while enacting some practices or
messages that say "this is a space for women," others
say "this is a space for everyone." It is this
ambiguity that people respond to, that makes it
impossible for either message to be successful. From
this perspective, Allen, calling to see if he could
come in for lunch is perfectly understandable. It may
seem preposterous to organizational members because the
ambiguity is not clear to them, but the aspects of the
message that qualify the situation, that makes it
perfectly okay for Allen to come in for lunch can
hardly be evident to Allen in light of the ambiguity.
Organizational goals are <u>both</u> separatist and nonseparatist, and this emerges in decision-making
interactions with patrons and most aspects of organization enactment.

According to Giddens, radical change "typically
emerges from contradictions that are opaque, repressed,
and dispersed throughout the system."[22] In this case
these descriptors <u>do</u> characterize the emergence of
contradictions in Twenty Rue Jacob, but the organization failed to change in a way that provided for its
continuation.

Repression

Repression or adherence to one position while
ignoring the contradictory alternative, serves to
stifle contradiction. Putnam says that "efforts to
merge a contradiction into a creative alternative, to

expose organizational traps and to view the situation from 'both the inside and outside' emancipate the system and its members."[23] What is occurring in Twenty Rue Jacob is that organizational members enact behaviors that either implicitly or explicitly adhere to one side of the contradiction or the other. This partitioning which allows members to only deal with one alternative at a time leads to "withdrawal from the scene. . . consistently repression of evolving changes and can result in the dissolution of work relationships, work units, and even organizations."

Partitioning, acknowledging only one alternative at a time, allows organization members more statements within one alternative which would never be entertained in another. "Let's get capitalistic," or "well, sisterhood is fine, but we need to make some money here," are legitimate within the business alternative, but not the ideological alternative.

The nature of the business in the context in which it is operating is contradictory. It cannot "be a business" and "be separatist" at the same time. It cannot "be political" and serve a "nonpolitical" clientele. Despite the strategies developed by organizational members to manage the contradictions, the primary contradictory situation required interdependence and integration to be successful and organizational members were unsuccessful in merging the alternatives.

Repression can and does work in organizations. If an organization is too tuned to the environment, it will be subject to the whims of everyone that impinges on it.[24] Organizations cannot be afraid to be identified if they are to remain stable and viable. Adaptation to environment may not mean 'sealing out' as

much as it means de-emphasizing some organizational
aspects in order to emphasize others to meet specific
situations at specific times. This is evident in the
Rue in the political nature of things. Repressing the
business aspects of the organization and emphasizing
politicalizing the community may have resulted in an
increased awareness of community obligation and
ultimately, an increase in business.

Starbuck contends that organizations that cannot
entertain competing ideologies are unable to adapt to
their environment and wither and die.[25] This provides
one possible explanation for the death of Twenty Rue
Jacob. Competing ideologies could not be entertained.
The management of contradiction became the only viable
option. Organizational members did develop strategies
to manage and explain the contradictions that arose in
their enactment of the business, but the ideology or at
least the social arrangements which arose from its
enactment, constrained the business and limited
transformation enough that radical change was not
possible and the business eventually had to close.

Conclusions

Putnam's paper claims to offer a starting point for
"weaving contradictions, conflicts, and problem solving
into a labyrinth that can effectively transform
organizational realities."[26] It provides a way of
examining the complexities of messages and meaning as
they impact on organizational change. With continued
research perhaps, she says, we can discover how
organizations pull themselves out of "self-made
quagmires by their own bootstraps."[27]

This dissertation has been aimed at showing how
some organizations cannot pull themselves out. In this
organization, contradictions were system-destructive,

rather than system integrative, because the ideology
was more important than the continuance of the organization - the organizational goals were more
important than the organization. Organizational
members did develop strategies to manage contradictions
in the places it emerged, but failed to integrate those
contradictions into the existing structure.

Both Putnam and Benson, while they are aiming at
different ends in their treatments of contradiction,
link organizational success with the continuance of the
organization. Benson views the aim of dialectical
organizational analysis as a concern with "conditions
under which people may reconstruct organizations and
establish social formations in which continuous reconstruction is possible."[28] The issues he addresses,
such as the humanization of work processes, are radical
structuralist in nature. The aim of analysis from
Putnam's perspective begins with understanding "the
complexities of messages and meanings as they impact on
organizational change"[29] but still ends with the aim of
discovering how organizations can overcome contradictions. These perspectives, as well as traditional
approaches to organizations proceed from the assumption
that the resultant structure is the central feature of
an organizing process.

To simply say that the contradictions were system
destructive and the business failed is not particularly
useful here, because it ignores the troublesome logical
problem presented by the concept of organizational
death. It assumes that if organizational members had
been 'successful' in managing contradiction and the
ideology had been less constraining, continuous
construction would have been possible and the organization would have been successful at least in remaining a

viable business entity. As it was, because the
organization died, it failed. I see this assumption as
problematic, because it does not deal with the question
of organizational integrity. At what point in undergo-
ing change does the organization cease to exist. As
Herbert Kaufman, in his work on organizational change
says, "How many changes can an organization make before
it is regarded as a totally new organization?"[30] Had
organizational members defined and redefined the
ideology to accommodate the contradictions, at what
point would the Rue have ceased to be the Rue?

On April 23, 1984 Twenty Rue Jacob conducted a
moving sale and the business closed down by 4:00 that
afternoon. On one wall inside the coffeehouse Alex
hung a large sign on which was the following message:
"Women of the Salt Lake City community - We won!"
Organizational members speculated on the possible
meanings.

One organizational member said to me "It's a
contradiction - it sounds like the kind of thing you
say before you give in to ultimate change." This
explanation is based on the assumption of success as
continuance. There is, however, an alternative
explanation, based on the assumption that success can
have different meanings for organizational members than
continuance, and that is that organizations can still
meet their goals, but ultimately fail in the traditional sense. This was very definitely the case at Twenty
Rue Jacob. Organizational members went along very
successfully accomplishing their goal "to provide a
place for women," but their goal was inconsistent with
business success. They met their goal, but still
failed. They 'won' because they accomplished the
original purpose of the organization. Some organiza-

tional members may regard the effort as a failure, but Alex preferred a different explanation. From her perspective, while the need was there, the Rue would somehow continue. She reconciled the contradictory elements by not seeing the two organizational goals as working against each other. If the need was really there in any significant respect, then the support would be there: if it was not, then that meant to her that its time was over, its organizational task accomplished. On the ideological level she saw the business not as a failure, but as a completed task. It succeeded on one level, even if it failed on the other.

In her closing letter, published in the Women Aware Newsletter, Alex said:

> If there were a need for 'the Rue,' someone from the community would have come forth to continue. Inasmuch as no one has at this time, it seems clear that Twenty Rue Jacob is no longer meeting the needs of this community. Perhaps something like 'the Rue' will exist in the future when the time is right.
>
> We need to give ourselves positive strokes for the three years we had with the Rue. We did what we knew how, the best we knew how. As Debbie Lempke writes in her song "Nicole" (Berkeley Women's Music Collective)
>> "but I know now, what I didn't know then
>> That you do know how, but you gotta know when."[31]

CHAPTER SIX

ENDNOTES

[1]J. Kenneth Benson, "Organizations: A Dialectical View," <u>Administrative Science Quarterly</u>, March 1977, Vol. 22, p. 1.

[2]J. Kenneth Benson, p. 1.

[3]Linda L. Putnam, "Contradictions and Paradoxes in Organizations," in L. Thayer and O. Wiio, <u>Explaining Organizations</u> (New York: Ablex Publishers, 1984), p. 2.

[4]Linda Putnam, p. 27.

[5]J. Kenneth Benson, p. 3.

[6]Linda Putnam, p. 3.

[7]W. B. Pearce and V. E. Cronen, <u>Communication, Action and Meaning</u> (New York: Praeger, 1980).

[8]Karl Weich, <u>The Social Psychology of Organizing</u> (Reading, MA: Addison-Wesley, 1979).

[9]Linda Putnam, p. 2.

[10]Linda Putnam, p. 5.

[11]Linda Putnam, p. 19.

[12]Linda Putnam, p. 21.

[13]Interview with a collective member in the Rue (8/5/83).

[14]Linda Putman, p. 21.

[15]J. Kenneth Benson, p. 14.

[16]K. Krippendorf, Paradox and Information, paper presented at the annual convention of the International Communication Association, Boston, May 1982.

[17]A. Dale, "Interface Issues," in R. Paybe and C. Cooper (eds.) Groups at Work (New York: John Wiley and Sons, 1981.

[18]G. Zeitz, "Interorganizational Dialectics," Administrative Science Quarterly, 1980, 25, p. 72-88.

[19]Lucia Valeska, "The Future of Female Separatism," in Building Feminist Theory: Essays From Quest (New York: Longman, Inc., 1981) p. 20-31.

[20]Linda Putnam, p. 22.

[21]Linda Putnam, p. 11.

[22]A. Giddens, Central Problems in Social Theory (Berkeley, California: University of California Press, 1979.)

[23]Linda Putnam, p. 12.

[24]Linda Putnam, p. 26.

[25]William Starbuck, "Congealing Oil: Inventing Ideologies to Justify Acting Ideologies Out," Journal of Management Studies, 19, 1982.

[26]Linda Putnam, p. 8.

[27]Linda Putnam, p. 22.

[28]J. Kenneth Benson, p. 18.

[29]Linda Putnam, p. 3.

[30]Herbert Kaufman, Change in Organizations (New York: Harper and Row, 1976).

[31]Women Aware Newsletter

APPENDIX

This appendix is an ethnographic description of a day spent at Twenty Rue Jacob. Its purpose is to provide the reader with a situational context for the interaction examined and analyzed in this study.

I pulled into the back parking lot at 10:50. It was a crisp fall morning and I made a mental note that the lot really needed sweeping, the same kind of mental note I had been making all summer about the weeds along the side of the building. I wondered what kind of a day it would be. Days at the Rue seem to fall into three categories. The days I liked the best were those heavily loaded with people; a constant stream of traffic in and out - people you knew, people you didn't. Sometimes they purchased something, but most often these days were primarily socially-oriented. We would sell a lot of cups of coffee, some lunches and maybe a record or two. The women would greet each other warmly with hugs and smiles and catch up on the news of each others lives. Some would come in to check the bulletin board and posters for local activities, others to check out the current stock of books, or to see who was there; but mostly they came to pass time with one another, to find a friendly face. It was like checking in at home to see what was going on, what was planned. I always left after these days feeling full and warm.

Other days were heavy business days. There was really no way to predict when one of these would come

along, but it wasn't often enough. Someone might come
in from Southern Utah or Wyoming and stock up on books
and records. Someone else might come in and look for a
birthday gift and leave with several books, a record
and a piece of pottery. Occasionally, two women might
come in looking for a piece of jewelry for one or the
other of them. These days were exciting because there
was a sense of keeping 'ones head above water,' but
often they were not social days. One reason for this
is that if things seemed busy, if whoever was working
was scurrying around trying to keep up with the phone,
the food and the bookstore, the women who came in
usually understood that it was not going to be a day
for visiting. They would have a cup of coffee or a
bite to eat and leave. The woman who was working
seemed to serve as a social coordinator, introducing
people who didn't know one another or just getting the
interaction going. When she couldn't, those warm
chatty days sometimes didn't develop unless several
people who knew each other happened to come in at the
same time.

The third kind of day was far too frequent. These
were empty days filled only with hours of waiting for
customers or friends to come through the door. Few
people appeared and when they did, they didn't linger.
These were the times when the women of the Rue would
talk about 'not being needed' or 'not being
appreciated' and about 'giving up.' On these kinds of
days I would often wonder if the Rue existed more for
the women who owned and ran it than for the community.
I dreaded days like that. It was even worse when one
of the collective members would call and ask how things
were going and I'd have to say, "It's pretty quiet." I
prayed that it wouldn't be like that today. A few

months ago, I would have arrived at 10:30 to set things
up before the opening at 11:30, but after too many days
of not seeing anyone come in until noon or after, it
seemed fruitless to arrive so early.

I came in up the cement ramp in the back and locked
the door behind me, switched out the outside lights and
plugged in the coffee machine so it could be warming
up. My first thought at walking into the kitchen in
the morning was to check and see if Louanne had been
in. She often came in to purchase groceries that might
be needed for the day before she went to work. Usually
there were telltale signs; the coffee machine was
already on, a bag of groceries or fresh bakery bread
was setting on the counter, or the outside lights were
already off. It somehow made you feel good to know she
had already checked in and that things were set for the
day. Even when several people arrived at once the
standard question at the beginning of the day was
always, "Did Louanne come in?" Sometimes there was a
rush around the corner to Safeway to pick up something
that had been left off the list the night before or to
cover things if she hadn't been able to come in. This
morning Louanne had been there. Fresh bread from the
bakery and a receipt were setting on the counter.

I opened the refrigerator and got out the ceramic
mug in which the till money and keys to the jewelry
case were kept. Sometimes the mug was well hidden
behind milk and cheese and it took a minute to locate
it. More often it was simply set on a shelf on the
inside of the refrigerator door. I counted out the $35
in singles, fives and change and put them in the old
grey cash drawer. Sometimes there were a couple of
extra dollars to compensate for the large bills. Other
times money was missing, either because Louanne used

money rather than write a check for the groceries of
because someone had needed a few dollars and replaced
it with a check of IOU. Sometimes there was less money
and no explanation, although someone always mentioned
later, "Oh, I needed $10. It was an emergency." The
money was always replaced. Mostly, people were
considerate of one another when that happened, but I
tended to become more panicky about it than anyone
else. Not because the money wasn't there, but because
I couldn't bear the thought of being caught without
change for someone. A till of $35 even made me
nervous. Everyone else seemed to take it in stride. I
complained once and Alex said, "Honey, there were days
we didn't even have a dollar in the till and made out
fine." After that, I felt a little more secure. There
was a credit union about two doors down where we often
went to get change. Sometimes, if the place was
crowded and you were alone, a trusted customer would
volunteer for the errand.

After I sorted the money into the drawer, I headed
into the bookstore. A flat wooden jewelry case with an
acrylic top sets on a short counter at the back of the
store. I reached into a metal cupboard in the office
and pulled out a coffee can where the jewelry was
hidden each night. It takes several minutes each
morning to separate and arrange the jewelry in the
case, but none of the jewelry, even the less expensive
pieces, has been kept out on display overnight since
the series of robberies eighteen months ago. Even when
stock is low, the jewelry is faithfully hidden and
redisplayed every morning. Collective members rarely
complain about the hassle involved. The stock of late
had been primarily silver because gold items are so
expensive. The design of the rings, charms and

earrings was distinctly feminist or contained lesbian
symbols: Women's symbols, double women's symbols,
labyris', and crystals.

The case was kept locked and was only opened when
customers wanted a closer look. Jewelry was one of the
more expensive items in the store and it was obvious
when women came in to buy it that it was a special
purchase for them - a birthday gift for themselves, a
friend or a lover. Sometimes the selection of a piece
involved a discussion of how blatant a particular
symbol was and where one could and could not wear it.
Carefully arranging the small pieces and tiny price
tags was far from my favorite chore.

Women's music played in the background all day
long. One speaker was located in the bookstore and one
in the dining room. Artists, such as Crus Williamson,
Holly Near, and Meg Christian, and groups, such as
Alive and Sweet Honey in the Rock, were particularly
popular. Most of the lyrics were either lesbian or
political in nature. Occasionally, if Louanne was
working, she would turn on the radio or she might even
put on Flashdance or a Michael Jackson album.
Sometimes people jokingly teased or rebuked her for
playing "cock rock" but she usually ignored them.
Lately, we had been playing some instrumental music,
mainly Fresh Aire tapes. The day was constantly
interrupted by the necessity of having to change or
adjust the music, but it was rarely a chore. Customers
often made requests or got tired of a particular tape
and requested a change of pace. Today, I put on a
newly released tape, Lifeline - Holly Near and Ronnie
Gilbert and adjusted the volume.

This 'setting-up' ritual each morning was the same
for whomever was working. It was almost always filled

with some excitement and a sense of possibility, even
though most days were far from exciting in terms of
sales, Rue members seemed energized by the woman-
oriented environment.

A day spent in Twenty Rue Jacob could be organized
around the people who came in. Concrete business
tasks, such as inventory, bill-paying, doing book
orders, even selling, were peripheral to discrete
social events.

At about 10:55 a solemn face appeared in the front
window. It was Ann and when she saw me she smiled and
waved. I got my keys, unlocked the front door and
flipped the open sign. Then, while she came in and
settled at the counter I put on the coffee. Ann, a
regular customer, was unemployed and came in at least
twice a week, sometimes spending as much as five or six
hours sitting at the counter and passing the time of
day with people who came in.

We exchanged a few words of greeting. I poured her
some coffee and she settled to read the paper, while I
went into the kitchen to cut up sandwich makings for
the day. You could never be sure you would need much
of it, but it was always prepared in case of a 'lunch
rush.' Most of the time there was no rush as such, but
rather a steady stream of customers, many of them
wanting only a cup of coffee or a pen and paper to
leave a note. If it was a good day whoever was working
was kept constantly busy until about 3 o'clock, but
somehow it didn't seem in looking back on even those
good days, that really much business was conducted.

On this particular day there were a number of
people who dropped in to pick up tickets for a Cris
Williamson concert to be held at the University the
following Friday. Over the last couple of weeks we had

sold most of the tickets we had. About ten had been
set aside for women who were coming in from Denver or
Wyoming for the concert. It never ceased to amaze the
women of the Rue how many women they had never seen
before showed up to buy tickets to women's concerts.
While Cris Williamson has a very large following of
antinuke people and conservationists, as well as
feminists, there is little doubt that the lesbian
orientation of much of her music draws a heavily
lesbian audience. Many of the women who came in to
purchase tickets, while unknown to the patrons who were
there at the time, were perceived as being lesbian.
Comments such as "Who was that?" or "Do you know them"
were often exchanged after they left.

While I was still in the kitchen preparing food,
Kathy came in the back door. She was dressed in jeans
and an expensive blazer and sweater and was carrying a
paper under her arm. Kathy worked for a local
engineering firm and hated her job because she "can't
stand structure." She was on an extended lunch hour.
Sometimes she came in on an errand from one building to
another. She greeted me cheerily and walked past me
and around to Ann's side of the counter. She dropped
the paper, front page up, in front of Ann. "See, if
women wanted they could take over the world in twenty
years. All they have to do is get their Ph.D.s in
environmental science." She motioned toward the front
page article with a banner head about the greenhouse
effect. "Ecosystems," she said, nodding. Last week
she had come in with an article on the 80-year-old
female geneticist who had won the nobel prize. She had
cut out the article and plinned it to the bulletin
board on the bookstore. "I'll have my usual," she
smiled. I went back to fix her a plain avocado and

jack cheese sandwich. There were several vegetarians among the customers and we had even gone through a stage when the menu was exclusively vegetarian.

The phone rang on and off all day. Once or twice it was an inquiry about a particular book; more often it was a call for Alex, one of the owners. By the end of the day, I had eight messages for her ranging from a call from a book distributor about a returned check to a call from her mother. Another call was from someone at the Phoenix Institute asking if we'd like to do the food for a fund raiser they were having.

Kelly came in for lunch. She was one of the owners and spent a lot of time in the business, particularly lately. She was doing graduate work at the University and when her classes for the day were over she would come in for lunch. Often Jane, the woman she lived, with would come in, too. Jane worked for the state and her lunch hours were her own to structure into her work day. Kelly always got there earlier than Jane and usually stayed considerably longer, sometimes a good portion of the afternoon.

Kelly and I were afflicted with a similar obsession for awhile. Neither one of us could seem to stay away from the Rue. Not that this obsession had never afflicted anyone else. It just seemed to be afflicting both of us at the same time. Actually for her this was an ongoing obsession that had started sometime before when she was a volunteer. I always loved it when she was there at the same time because there was always plenty to talk about.

Among the more notable events of this particular day was two young women who came in early afternnon and ordered two cups of coffee. They were obviously upset and isolated themselves from the few people gathered

around the counter by selecting a booth in the corner.
When I went to refill their coffee cups they asked if
the could speak to Alex so I called her from the
kitchen where she had been. She pulled up a chair and
sat down. The two women held hands across the table as
they talked. Both appeared very young, very attractive
and were wearing dresses and high heels. I remember
mentally classifying them as bank tellers or
secretaries when they first came in.

They needed the name of a lawyer, they said, who
would be sensitive to their problem. They were being
threatened by the ex-husband of one of the women, who
said he would take the child away if they continued to
see each other. They were confused and afraid and
needed help. The one with the child sat quietly while
the other did all the talking. Alex wrote a name and
number on a piece of paper and gave it to them. They
sat awhile longer, ate a sandwich and then left.

Kim arrived about 2:30. It was always a high spot
in the day when she stopped in because she was bright
and cheery and fun to pass time with. She was checking
to see how pottery sales were going. Kim did the
majority of the pottery items in the shop and once a
year at the beginning of December she and the jeweler
had a 'show' and served wine and cheese at the opening.
Lately she had purchased a truck that turned out to be
a 'lemon' and so a lot of her talk seemed to focus on
the trials and tribulations of an undependable vehicle.
This time, however, she had other more relationship-
based concerns on her mind. Kim always ordered a
vegetarian sandwich and I always put on extra avocado.
Lately, Kim and I had been having some long talks, but
today there were too many people around and so we just
sort of gave each other encouraging smiles and she ate

and left.

At one point, when it was quiet, I asked Kathy to
do the 'dyke' thing. This was always met by an
encouraging audience even though most people had
witnessed it before. Kathy had tired of it sometime
ago, but always rallied to do it one more time. During
the summer of 1983, Salt Lake City had problems with
flooding. The city's drainage system could not handle
the heavy spring run-off. Large numbers of people
turned out to build sandbag dikes and form man-made,
directed rivers through the city. Radio announcers
often made reference to the six-foot dikes directing
the water through the city and around the park. It had
been one hot summer day when the flooding was at its
worst that Kathy had turned on the radio to hear the
news and giggled to herself when the announcer
described the effectiveness of the 'dikes.'

"What's so funny?" someone had asked her.

"Well, it's just that whenever they say that I get
this image."

"Like what?"

Well, Kathy paused then ran around the counter into
the center of the room. Everyone stopped eating and
watched.

She drew herself up tall, lifted her arm and
pointed her finger, and with a stern expression on her
face, in short, quick jerks moved her arm as if giving
cool, well-defined directions to some menacing force.

That first performance was met with enthusiasm.
Women were hysterical with laughter, but the response
lessened with each subsequent telling. It had never,
however, failed to get a good laugh and it got one this
time.

The last hour or so of the day was always the most

difficult. Usually this was from 4 or 4:30 to 6:00.
Rarely was there any socializing at all and only
occasionally did anyone stop in to buy anything, but we
stayed open for the benefit of women who worked all day
and stopped in after work to pick up a record or book
or have a cup of coffee. Usually, however, whoever was
working spent that time sitting and waiting for the day
to end. Today, I started cleaning up and putting
things away at 5:00. It was a bit of a gamble in case
anyone came in and wanted to see the jewelry, but by
5:15 I took the chance and put the jewelry back into
the coffee can in which it was kept. Than after
cleaning the kitchen and closing out the till, I sat in
a booth and read a copy of Off Our Backs, a radical
feminist newspaper.

When 6:00 arrived, I turned the open sign in the
front window to closed, turned out the inside lights
and turned on the outside lights and let myself out the
back door.

SELECTED BIBLIOGRAPHY

Anderson, James A. Teaching Qualitative Methods. A paper presented at the AEJ Convention, Athens, Ohio, 1982.

Bacca Zinn, Maxine. "Field Research in Minority Communities: Ethical, Methodological and Political Observations by an Insider." Social Problems, Vol. 27, No. 2, December 1979.

Benson, J. Kenneth. "Organizations: A Dialectical View." Administrative Science Quarterly, March 1977, Vol. 22, p. 1.

Berger, Peter and Luckman, Thomas. The Social Construction of Reality. Garden City, New Jersey: Doubleday and Co., Inc., 1966.

Brandow, Karen. Jim McDonnell, and Vocations for Social Change. No Bosses Here. Boston, MA: Alyson Publications, 1981.

Burrell, Gibson and Morgan, Gareth. Social Paradigms and Organizational Analysis. London: Heinemann, 1979.

Dale, A. "Interface Issues." In Groups at Work. New York: John Wiley and Sons, 1981.

Daly, Mary. Gyn/Ecology: The Metaethics of Radical Feminism. Boston: Beacon Press, 1978 pp. 381-82.

Freeman, Jo. The Politics of Women's Liberation. New York: Longman, 1975.

Frye, Marilyn. The Politics of Reality: Essays in Feminist Theory. New Work: The Crossing Press, 1983, p. 95.

Geertz, Clifford. "Blurred Genres: The Refiguration of Social Thought." American Scholar, Spring 1980, p. 166.

Giddens, A. Central Problems in Social Theory. Berkeley, CA: University of California Press, 1979.

Gregory Lewis, Sasha. Sunday's Women: A Report on Lesbian Life Today. Boston, MA: Beacon Press, 1979.

Hayes, Joseph J. "Lesbians, Gay Men, and their 'Languages.'" In Gayspeak. Ed. by James W. Chesebro. New York: The Pilgrim Press, 1981, pp. 28-42.

Jaggar, Alison. "Political Philosophies of Women's Liberation." In Feminism and Philosophy. Ed. Veterling-Braggin, Frederick A. Elliston, and Jan English. Titowa, New Jersey: Littlefield, Adams, 1977.

Kaufman, Herbert. Change in Organizations. New York: Harper and Row, 1976.

Kimball, Gayle. "Defining Women's Culture: An Interview with Robin Morgan." In Women's Culture: The Women's Renaissance of the Seventies. Boston: The Scarecrow Press, Inc., 1981, p. 30.

Krippendorf, K. Paradox and Information. A paper presented at the annual convention of the International Communication Association, Boston, May 1982.

Legorn, Lisa and Parker, Katherine. Woman's Worth: Sexual Economics and The World of Women, Boston: Routledge & Kegan Paul, 1981.

Lesbianism and the Women's Movement. Ed. by Nancy Myron and Charlotte Bunch. Baltimore, MD: Diana Press, 1975, p. 30.

Meyer, Alan. "How Ideologies Supplant Formal Structures and Shape Responses to Environments." Journal of Management Stujdies, No. 19, 1982.

Morgan, Gareth. "Paradigms, Metaphors and Puzzle Solving in Organization Theory." Administrative Science Quarterly, Vol. 25, No. 4, Dec. 1980, pp. 605-622.

Mudd, Karen. "Lesbian Separatism: Then and Now." Off Our Backs, August/September 1983, p. 10.

New York Radicalesbians, "The Woman-Identified Woman." Lesbians Speak Out. Ed. by the Women's Press Collective, New York, 1971, p. 53.

Painter, Dorothy. "Recognition Among Lesbians in Straight Settings." In Gayspeak. Ed. by James Cheesbro. New York: The Pilgrim Press, 1981, pp. 68-79.

Pearce, W. B. and Cronen, V. E. Communication, Action and Meaning. New York: Praeger, 1980.

Putnam, Linda L. "Contradictions and Paradoxes in Organizations." In L. Thayer and O. Wiio, Explaining Organizations. New York: Ablex Publishers, 1984.

Putnam, Linda. "Paradigms for Organizational Communication Reseasrch: An Overview and Synthesis." Western Journal of Speech Communication, Vol. 46, No. 2, Spring 1982, p. 200.

Putnam, Linda. "The Interpretive Perspective: An Alternative to Functionalism." In Communication and Organizations: An Interpretive Approach. Ed. Linda Putnam and Michael Pacanowsky. Beverly Hills: Sage Publications, Inc., 1983, pp. 31-54.

Rich, Adrienne. "Notes for a Magazine: What Does Separatism Mean?" Sinister Wisdom, 18, 1981, pp. 83-91.

Ritzer, G. "Sociology: A Multiple Paradigm Science." American Sociologist, No. 10, 1975, pp. 156-167.

Rook, June. "The Need for a Lesbian History," WIN: Peace and Freedom Thru Nonviolent Action, June 26, 1985, p. 18.

Russ, Joanna. "Power and Helplessness in the Women's Movement." In Sinister Wisdom, No. 18, Fall 1981.

Simon, Linda. The Biography of Alice B. Toklas. New York: Avon books, 1978, p. 160.

Sisterhood is Powerful. Ed. Robin Morgan, New York: Random House, 1970.

Starbuck, William. "Congealing Oil: Inventing Ideologies to Justify Acting Ideologies Out." Journal of Management Studies, 19, 1982.

Strine, Mary S. and Pacanowsky, Michael. "How to Read Interpretive Accounts of Organizational Life: The 'Positionality' of the Researcher as an Informing Principle," unpublished manuscript, University of Utah, 1984.

Swenson, D. L. "On the Use of Symbolist Insight in the Study of Political Communication." Human Communication Research, No. 8, 1982, pp. 379-382.

Turner, Victor. Foreward. In Number Our Days. Barbara Myerhoff. New York: Simon and Schuster, 1978.

Valeska, Lucia. "The Future of Female Separatism." In Building Feminist Theory: Essays From Quest. Ed. Charlotte Brunch. New York: Longman, Inc., 1981, pp. 20-31.

Weick, Karl E. "Organizational Communication: Toward a Research Agenda." In Communication and Organizations: An Interpretive Approach. Eds. Linda Putnam and Michael Pacanowsky. Beverly Hills: Sage Publications, 1983.

Weick, Karl. The Social Psychology of Organizing. Reading, MA: Addison-Wesley, 1979.

Zeitz, G. "Interorganizational Dialectics," Administrative Science Quarterly, 1980, 25, pp. 72-88.

Zey-Farrell, M. and Aiken, M. "Introduction to Critiques of Dominant Perspectives." Complex Organizations: Critical Perspectives. Eds. M. Zey-Farrell and M. Aiken. Glenview: Illinois: Scott, Foresman, 1981.